MW00769136

"For the Glory of God"

Called by the Gospel
To China
By Mark Czanderna

Quotations:
Allowed without permission when author & publisher credited

New Edition

Copyrighted 2021
LuLu Publishing Company

ISBN 978-1-7947-0372-8

Contact the author 21stcenturyjeremiah@gmail.com

Introduction

1988, Guangzhou City, China: Lydia shared her testimony with me, "My birthday was June 10. I was dreading this day. I didn't know how to face it. Then, a missionary who spoke at our house church came to visit us on June 10. I was so happy. Today, July 3, would've been my husband's birthday. I was also dreading this day, but now, God has brought you and your family to us. I know this is Jesus. I am so happy today."

As I typed Lydia's testimony, I realized her birthday was on the 15th anniversary of my father's death. I had said to the Lord during my father's funeral that I wanted HIM (the Lord) to use my life to comfort the bereaved with the Gospel. I felt at that time that God would either call me to China or to Africa or both. Here I was in China, comforting a bereaved widow. Our Lord answered the silent prayer that I prayed at age 13.

The joy of leading someone from a different culture to Jesus is an exceedingly great joy. For us this joy outweighed our need for certain types of food, our need to communicate in English and our need to live in a familiar location.

Our children, Grace, Glory, Andrew, and Mercy were vital to our mission to China. I originally composed this book for them. A friend expressed interest to read it, so I re-edited it for a wider audience. During the re-editing process, I prayed that our Lord Jesus would use this book to inspire you, the reader, to share the good news of Christ's love with others.

Table of Contents

~ Chapter 1 ~
Called by the Gospel (Pre-China Days)

As mentioned in the introduction, I was deeply comforted by the Gospel when I heard it preached at my father's funeral at age 13. Four years after that, the church that I attended held an Evangelism Explosion training. Once again, the Gospel came through for me. As I was memorizing 1 John 2:2, I realized that the Gospel wasn't just for the saints around me, it was for me too.

I John 2:2 says, "And He Himself is the propitiation for our sins, and not for ours only but also for the whole world." I interpreted the "our sins" as applying to the saints in my church, and "the world" as applying to me because I was still very worldly. Through this passage, the Holy Spirit assured me that the sacrifice of Christ on the cross applied to me. My sins were forgiven by God, and I was saved. I would go to heaven when I died thanks to Jesus! Hallelujah!

The Lord wants us to be assured that our salvation is a done deal. 1 John 5:13 says, "These things I have written to you... that you may know that you have eternal life." John 5:24 says, "Most assuredly, I say to you, he who hears My word and believes in Him who sent Me has everlasting life, and shall not come into judgment, but has passed from death into life."

The Evangelism Explosion (EE) training classes that I attended went on for several weeks. By the time, we were paired up to do visitations, I was well prepared to share the Gospel. I had learned the contents of the Gospel. I had memorized key passages

1

for presenting the Gospel. I had memorized Gospel illustrations. I had memorized conversational icebreakers. I had learned how to respond to hard questions about God and the Bible. I had memorized EE's two diagnostic questions.

The two diagnostic questions are designed to help people to see who they are trusting in to save them. The first question is, "Have you come to the place in your life where you know that if you died, you would go to heaven?" The second question is, "If you were to stand before God and he were to ask you, 'Why should I let you into my heaven?' What would you say?"

During the evangelistic outreaches, I was blessed to be paired with our church elder Terry Page. He was filled with the Holy Spirit. He loved God and people. The Lord gave us success in presenting the Gospel to people whom we visited. Terry supported our overseas mission from beginning to end.

In 1979, the Lord brought me to the place where I gladly surrendered my life for His use. After that, He opened the door for me to enjoy a Christian education at Concordia Teachers College. While there, I learned the importance of distinguishing the function of the Law from the function of the Gospel.

C.F.W. Walther wrote, "The Law tells us what we are to do. No such instruction is contained in the Gospel. On the contrary, the Gospel reveals to us only what God is doing. The Law is speaking concerning our works; the Gospel, concerning the great works of God." [1] So, the goal of any Gospel presentation is to help people see that what we bring to God is sin and failure to reflect His glory. What God brings to us is salvation based on the merits of His Son Jesus Christ. Jesus lived a sinless life in human flesh, was crucified, buried, and resurrected on the third day. In this way, He proved that He is the Messiah. His grace is what sets Christianity apart from all other religions. Walther wrote, "Try and realize this important distinction. All religions contain portions of the Law. But of the Gospel not a particle is found anywhere except in the Christian religion." [2]

While I was at Concordia, I read a pamphlet by Christian singer and composer Keith Green entitled, "Why YOU Should Go to the Mission Field." In this pamphlet, Keith provided eight reasons why I should go to the mission field, and fifteen common excuses people make for not going. This tract hit me like a bolt of lightning. Would I be content to pastor people in the US, or would I take the Gospel to those who lacked a Gospel witness?

Keith wrote, "There are over 2,700,000,000 people who have never heard the Gospel at all, and there are only 5,000 to 7,000 missionaries worldwide, working directly with these totally unreached groups of people. [3] That means there is approximately one missionary for every 450,000 of these people! There are over

---

[1] Walther, C.F.W., The Proper Distinction Between Law and Gospel, Just & Sinner, 1467 Walnut Ave., Brighton, IA, 52540, (c) 2014, p. 14-15
[2] Ibid
[3] Once Around Jericho by Roberta Winter; William Carey Library Publishing.

16,000 different and distinct cultures and people-groups - even whole countries, where not one single church is in existence. [4] There are 7,010 distinct living languages, and 5,199 of them still have no Bible or Scripture translations available in their own language! [5] Do these figures move you at all? Does it matter to you that an estimated 80,000 unsaved people die every day (approximately 3,333 every hour...55 people every single minute!) to face the judgment seat of Christ? [6]

In January 1981, Dave Russert informed me of a new student. Her name was Sherry. He was very impressed with her. His goal was to win her to himself. Thankfully, God had a different spouse for Dave. Sherry was God's choice for me.

The more I got to know Sherry the more I loved her. What impressed me the most about Sherry was that when we talked, our conversations were centered in Christ. After so many meals together in the cafeteria, after so many hallway conversations and after praying together on numerous occasions, I discovered that being away from her was painful. My heart literally ached for Sherry when I could not be with her. I wanted to marry her. I had absolutely no doubt that she was God's spouse for me. Sherry believed that she would go farther with the Lord with me in her life than she would without me.

---

[4] Ibid
[5] World Christian Encyclopedia by David Barrett.
[6] In the Gap, What It Means To Be A World Christian by Dave Bryant; pg. 121

Before Sherry and I married, I was the Residential Assistant for the foreign students who stayed in Lindemann Hall. I enjoyed working with these students. They were from the Middle East, Africa, and South Korea. At first, my closest friend was a pastor from Chad, Africa. Later, I befriended a Nigerian man named Jean-Pierre. He believed in and professed Christ. He was baptized. After Jean-Pierre, I befriended a Korean couple named Jeong and Misook Gho. They became my daily prayer partners. Jeong encouraged me to pray for the People's Republic of China (PRC). He said that the PRC desperately needed missionaries. Sherry was also praying for me to be a missionary.

Sherry is a great listener. She went through a difficult season in her life when she was 12 years old. She found relief from her suffering when she was counseled at a Nazarene church to praise the Lord during difficulties. She still praises God daily.

Sherry and I were married on June 5, 1982. What a wonderful day! The theme of our wedding ceremony was "Lift high the cross. The love of Christ proclaim. 'Till all the world adore His sacred Name." After we married, we started attending the Chinese Bible Church in Oak Park, Illinois.

While at the Chinese Bible Church, a member who was trained by Campus Crusade for Christ, spoke about discipleship. He urged us to obey God's calling on our lives. The people in this church spoke Cantonese, so I started learning Cantonese. Then one evening, they showed a movie. It was about the life of a missionary to China named Hudson Taylor. God used this movie to build our faith in Him that if we took the Gospel to the PRC, He would provide for us.

After we completed our bachelor's degrees, I did not go to seminary. Sherry did not become a Lutheran high school teacher. I had explored various options for taking the Gospel to the PRC. When I came across the name of a missionary sending agency named Christ is the Answer Ministries (CITA), I wrote to them. They invited us to join their ministry for three months, which we did. CITA was in El Paso, Texas. While there, we did evangelism in El Paso. We did ministry in Juarez, Mexico. Sherry served as an assistant manager in CITA's refugee house.

During our days with CITA, we were a part of a tent crusade ministry team. Our team was sent to Las Cruces, New Mexico. For two weeks we witnessed daily. Despite the coldness and threats of unbelievers, five people converted, nine Christians joined the ministry, and a Mormon lady was converted by Jesus.

Prior to the Las Cruces crusade, we evangelized the neighborhoods. We also shared the Gospel at a nearby university and a shopping mall. I was stung by a scorpion prior to the shopping mall outreach. I needed medical attention afterwards. The enemy tried to take me out, but God preserved me.

One day, while Sherry and I were talking to people about God, God spoke to us. This happened on the streets of El Paso near the border of Mexico. We were walking on a sidewalk. Sherry was telling me that she was concerned that her parents were worried about her and that she needed to call them. When we reached a street corner, a man dressed in suit stopped us and asked us, "Where have you been?" I asked him, "What do you mean." He turned to Sherry and said, "The Lord says to you that your parents are not worrying about you." Then, he said to both of us, "I saw you and you with Jesus in the sky with many children." How do you reply to such a declaration? We were stunned.

We did not plan to have children at that stage in our lives. We were concerned that if we did, we would relent to take the Gospel to the PRC. The Lord changed our perspective that day. In the days following that incident, the Lord helped us to see how He uses the children of missionaries to draw people to Himself.

After our three-month commitment with CITA ended, we opted to travel from El Paso to Los Angeles to check out the English Language Institute for China. Perhaps, the Lord would use this organization to send us overseas. CITA prepared us to be missionaries, but they were not able to send us to China.

While on our way to Los Angeles, we stopped in Las Cruces, New Mexico. We visited with Martha, her sister, and their children. We had picked them up almost every night during the Las Cruces tent crusade. We did a Bible study with them and prayed for them. Both Martha and her sister were beaten with belt buckles and molested by their brothers, and again, later, by their husbands. They were raising their five children together. They had physical and emotional scars from the beatings. They needed Jesus to heal them.

The next day we gave two hitchhikers a ride. One man was named Kris. He believed in Christ. The other man was named Jerry. Jerry had been on the road for seven years when he stopped at "Jesus House" in Tulsa, Oklahoma. The people at Jesus House provided Jerry six months of lodging, food, clothing, and Bible instruction. Teachers from a local Bible College provided free Bible lessons for the homeless. Jerry said a high percentage of the sojourners fell in love with the teachings of Jesus and began to share Scriptures with others. Jerry acquired a large vocabulary of Scriptures during his six months at Jesus House.

We towed our home behind our Gran Torino station wagon. It was a 12-foot camper that we had purchased in Indiana. It was our home while at CITA.

After arriving in Los Angeles, we located a Christian and Missionary Alliance (CMA) Church. Pastor Mark Searing of the CMA Church in El Paso provided us a letter of recommendation to take with us. This CMA church rented its facility and could not let us park our camper in their parking lot.

Thankfully, God provided a man to direct us to The Salvation Army. The Army provided us a parking space for our camper. They shared with us their electricity for our camper. They gave us an open-ended invitation to park in the lot.

On a Thursday evening, we attended a prayer meeting at the Ontario CMA Church. To our surprise many of the members had been missionaries. They comforted us. They were not surprised by what we had done in leaving everything to follow our calling. They were confident that God would bless us. They encouraged us. Two of the members invited us to park our camper near their apartment. They invited us to stay with them.

On a Friday, I visited the US Center of World Missions. A man associated with the Chinese World Mission Center gave us a free pass to attend a seminar on Chinese Awareness. The pass was worth $40. I attended the seminar. I learned that one out of three unbelievers in the world were Chinese, and that as many as 500 Chinese Christians shared one Bible in a village.

On our fourth day in California, Sherry was volunteering at the office of the English Language Institute for Chinese (ELIC). ELIC needed volunteers. We prayed about going to the PRC under their umbrella, but the Lord did not lead us this way.

After that time in California, we returned to Illinois where Sherry's parents lived. We were given the name of Larry Rice in St. Louis as an option for temporary service unto the Lord until the door to the PRC opened for us. Larry Rice was happy to put us to work. After a short training period, he sent us from St. Louis to Columbia, Missouri to establish and manage a New Life Evangelistic Center (NLEC). NLEC ministry involved personal evangelism, sheltering and relief item distribution.

Our Savior Jesus Christ provided for us donors to donate food and clothes. He provided for us financial supporters. Even our parents joined us in doing street corner ministry.

Throughout 1984, we worked hard to develop the NLEC ministry. By the end of the first quarter of 1985, we reported to

Larry that we had distributed massive amounts of food and clothing, 250 blankets, 100 checks of $35 for utility assistance, 113 kerosene or wood burning heaters, 73 weatherization kits, over 100 infant car seats and numerous cases of Bibles and devotional booklets. We shared God's Word with the applicants. Seven people professed Jesus Christ as their Savior. We provided emergency shelter for women, married couples, and children. We held worship services for the shelter guests on Saturday evenings.

Debbie and Clarence Williams were guests at our NLEC shelter. One day, Debbie had a seizure while standing on a ladder. She fell to the ground. Clarence called me from the hospital to tell me that their unborn child was dead. Upon receiving this news, we bowed our faces to the floor and prayed that God would raise their baby to life. The next day, Clarence told us that their baby revived and lived. They moved to Vancouver. After the baby was born, Clarence phoned to tell me that they named their baby Gabriel because he was their angel.

The Lord also did a miracle for a lady named Ronnie Bell. She came to us at a time when local foodbanks lacked meat. She told me that her child's doctor prescribed meat for her child because he was anemic. I told her that we had no meat. She asked me, "Then, what am I to do?" The Lord spoke to me, He said, "Tell Ronnie that she will have meat before the day is over." So, I told her. She wanted to know how God would provide. I told her that He did not tell me how but that He would surely supply her meat before the day was over.

We did not see Ronnie again until the next time she had a need. She needed help to prevent her electricity from being shut off. I asked her, "Ronnie, what happened on that day you needed meat?" She replied, "A neighbor bought a side of beef and could not get all the new meat into her freezer without getting rid some of the older meat that was still good. She gave us that older meat. We had a lot of meat." Then, the Lord told me to tell Ronnie, "The Lord says that your electricity will not be shut off." She doubted me because she already had received two cut-off notices from the power company. I told her not to worry. The power company granted her a third extension that day. A rare occurrence! Glory to God!

We prayed much while tending to the needs of a family of six. The Lord told Peter, "If you love Me, feed My lambs." We love the Lord, so we trusted Him to provide food for the lambs that He wanted us to feed. He did!

The family of six included two young man ages 29 and 24. Men were not allowed to stay in our women's and children's shelter, so I slept down in the ministry center with them. One man's name was Billy. He asked me a lot of questions about God. He was a Vietnam War veteran. He had a history of violence, but he followed me around writing down the Scriptures that I shared with him. He was about four inches taller than me. He had long hair. The Lord had urged us to feed His flock as an expression of love for Him. Jesus gave us willing spirits. Five of the six members of this family believed in Jesus were baptized. The only

11

reason one member was not baptized was that he came to faith after the baptism service ended, but he too believed!

I witnessed Christ's love in Sherry as she cooked for and spoke with the people in the shelter. I witnessed His love in our Christian volunteers as they denied themselves to help others in need. God had given them new hearts and new love for people.

Grace, our first child, was born on October 31 at the University of Missouri Hospital. When Sherry and Grace came home from the hospital, Sherry was exhausted. Grace started crying. I laid Grace on my chest and gently patted her on the back until she fell asleep. What a very special experience that was! We had our own baby. We named her Grace because she was born on Reformation Day. We did not give her a middle name because we knew that grace was sufficient.

Leading up to Grace's birth, God delivered us from trials by grace. The first trial was that I came down with mononucleosis in August. This illness started with a high fever of 104. The second trial was insufficient funds to pay my hospital bill. A social worker at the hospital asked me how I intended to pay my bill. I replied, "A little at a time." We had no insurance and less than a $100 to our name. So, although I was not better, I left the hospital. During the next 28 days I was bed-ridden. Sherry ran the shelter with the help of a volunteer named Bunny Walters. My medicine was the Word of God. I read the Bible from cover to cover. On the day that I finished reading the Bible, the Holy Spirit placed Numbers 10:9 and 2 Chronicles 13:13-18 on my heart.

"When you go to war in your land against the enemy who oppresses you, then you shall sound an alarm with the trumpets, and you will be remembered before the Lord, and you will be saved from your enemies." [7]

"Now, Jeroboam had sent troops around to the rear, so that while he was in front of Judah the ambush was behind them. Judah turned and saw that they were being attacked at both front and rear. Then, they cried out to the Lord. The priests blew their trumpets, and the men of Judah raised the battle cry. At the sound of their battle cry, God routed Jeroboam and all Israel before Abijah and Judah. The Israelites fled before Judah, and God delivered them into their hands. Abijah and his troops inflicted heavy losses on them, so that there were five hundred thousand casualties among Israel's able men. The Israelites were subdued on that occasion, and the people of Judah were victorious because they relied on the Lord, the God of their ancestors." [8]

Based on these passages, I wanted to sound a trumpet to the Lord. I called Sherry using the upstairs shelter telephone. She was in the downstairs ministry office. I said, "Sherry, can you bring a vacuum cleaner pipe upstairs for me? I want to blow a trumpet." She thought I wanted her to blow air into my throat and responded, "No!" But when I explained to her further what I intended to do, she brought it. I blew in the vacuum pipe seven times and shouted praise to God. At that moment, the boil in the

[7] Numbers 10:9 NIV
[8] 2 Chronicles 13:13-18 NIV

back of my throat burst and by night fall I could painlessly swallow again. My fever was gone. My strength returned.

The other trial for which I blew the "trumpet" was our debt. We owed $1,400 to the hospital due to my four-day stay. On top of this, the price tab for our baby's prenatal care and delivery at Mizzou University hospital was $3,000.

God won battles for us. The State legislature wanted the psychiatric care ward cleared of people who they deemed as exploiters of the system. They passed legislation to force these patients out. Ours was the only shelter in town, so the hospital started sending the homeless to us. Someone on the hospital's Board of Regents heard that we sheltered the homeless patients and asked the Board to cancel my $1,400 debt and to reduce the price tag for Sherry's prenatal care and delivery from $3,000 to $500. After they did that, a check arrived in the mail. The amount was $500. The Lord healed me. He paid our debts. Glory to God!

The Lord used our trials to grow our faith in His ability to provide for us on the mission field. Another miracle that sprung forth from my time of illness was the arrival of a woman who felt called to take over the leadership of the ministry. Praise the Lord!

After our time with the NLEC, we joined the Bible and Literacy League ministry in Hillsboro, Missouri. They did not send us to the PRC, but while there, the Lord led me to fast and pray for four days. After that fast, Pastor Frank Westfall of Living Faith Center in Ashland, Missouri, contacted me and connected me with the Director of Hong Kong (HK) Youth for Christ (YFC). His name was David Chu.

I wrote David Chu. He wrote back to me, "We can sense that you have a true burden for the Chinese. We also believe that the power of God will make the impossible possible. Your past experiences with witnessing, open-air concerts and food relief are assets that you can bring to the ministry."

"Prayer is the key to any work for God. I assure you that our programs are Scriptural. We try to present the Gospel through music, drama, and choreography with the goal of offering an opportunity to accept Christ. New converts are followed up."

"You mentioned a possible visit to Hong Kong with Lynn Haitz the director of the Bible and Literacy League (BALL). I encourage you to do so. This will be most beneficial to help you make further decisions. During that time, I would like to meet you personally and discuss our ministry approaches. If you can be flexible to live in a crowded family environment, and need accommodations, I can arrange for you to stay in homes. Let us continue to pray about your involvement in Hong Kong and China." Thus, our ministry in HK began.

~ Chapter 2 ~
Called by the Gospel (1985)

The prayers of God's people availed much. I arrived in
Hong Kong (HK) on June 25, 1985. The Lord graced both the
YFC leaders and myself with favor one towards another. They
were happy with me. I was happy with them. The Director David
Chu together with the Board of Advisors offered me the position
of Assistant Director. The goals they set for me were to assist the
director with administrative duties, liaison between overseas
visitors and local staff members, and to assist with evangelism
and discipleship. I accepted. Sherry arrived two months later with
baby Grace. Grace was less than 10-months-old.

The Lord used YFC to open many doors for me to share
the Gospel with people who did not know Jesus. For example, on
June 29, I had the opportunity to share at a Christian camp. 98%
of the teenagers were not Christians. They cursed, smoked and
were rowdy. The camp director said to me, "Don't feel bad if no
one responds to the Gospel."

Praise God for a powerful move of the Holy Spirit. I told
the teens of Christ's death, resurrection, ascension and second
coming. I shared with them what God hates from Psalm 5:4-5,
11:5 and 31:6. I gave an altar call. Few responded! But then I
prayed, "Holy Spirit get them!" A wind blew from behind me and
went over the teenagers. After that, about 20 hands went up.
These confessed Christ as their Lord and Savior.

16

A team of American Christians and I visited a home for juvenile delinquent boys. The Christians played basketball with the boys. I prayed. Before I knew it, three boys wanted to profess faith in Christ as their Lord and Savior. Praise the Lord!

When we arrived in HK, I did not expect to find so many lost souls. We had worshipped with Christians from HK while in the US. I believed that HK would be a launch pad for our mission to the PRC. However, the people were spiritually needy.

Only 4% of HK's six million people were Christians. Idols were everywhere. Apartments and businesses had idols. The five key idols were landlord idols; ancestor idols; wealth idols; General Kwan idols; and Guan Yin idols. Some people spent as much as $90 on paper houses, cars, and servants. These carefully made images of worldly wealth were set on fire inside metal bins on the sidewalks. This ceremony was done for dead relatives.

There were also festivals for the dead. August 29th was the "Ghost Festival." On this day, the tradition was that the gates of hell were open, and dead spirits were released. People burned "Hell Bank Notes" and incense for the dead. Psalm 106:36-37 compares idolatry with demon worship. There were Buddhist temples scattered throughout HK.

HK's crime rate was high. Apartment doors were shielded by iron gates and windows had steel bars. It was like living in a safe. Pornography was openly displayed on sidewalk newsstands. Prostitution signs were everywhere. It was reported that a schoolteacher quit his job to become a pimp. He acquired thirty

17

18-year-old girls in a month's time. Proverbs 7:13-30 states that the prostitute's room is the "room of hell."

The positives about HK were that the people believed in a spiritual world. Many believed that prosperity and poverty were directly affected by one's spiritual life. So, they were open-hearted to talk about spiritual matters.

YFC had access into many of HK's 450 high schools. They presented the Gospel via drama presentations, pantomimes, music, testimonies, and the preaching of God's Word. 50-100 new confessions of faith in Christ per week were not uncommon. YFC also had access to juvenile prisons where the Gospel was presented to boys between the ages of 14-19.

During the first five days of July 1985, I preached the Gospel at four schools. Over 1,000 young people professed faith in Christ during those meetings. 11 professed faith in Christ after I shared the Gospel with them one on one. Glory to God!

The Lord did miracles. He healed a baby boy after I prayed for him. The Lord healed an American soccer player. He was trying to outrun another player. While looking back, he failed to notice a concrete block on the boundary line. He tripped over the block and flew headfirst into a metal wall. This happened at a prison on an outlying island. It was a soccer game between a Christian American soccer team and Chinese prisoners. When the American player revived, he cried, "My arm! My leg are paralyzed!" The Holy Spirit assured me a that he would be healed. After some persuasion, I was granted permission to lay my hand on him and pray for him. As soon as I placed my hand on his leg, God's power healed him. He testified, "I'm better! I'm okay!" By the time an ambulance arrived, he was standing and walking. The prisoners cheered. He (Steve) went to the hospital. The doctor confirmed that he was uninjured. Not even a bump on his head!

By the time Sherry and Grace arrived in August of 1985, I had adjusted to oriental life. I knew my way around. I had made friends. I was fully occupied with missionary service. Sherry, on the other hand, experienced culture shock. Things went from bad to worse when she and Grace became ill. I was so pre-occupied with the mission that I did not pay much attention to her pleas to slow down. I was preaching the Gospel and Chinese people were believing in Christ. I assumed that if I faithfully preached the Gospel to lost souls that God would take care of my family.

Sherry experienced unfamiliar pain and sensations due to her illness. Director David Chu's wife watched her at his home. His wife, Louise, was a medical doctor.

Besides dealing with culture shock and illness, Sherry had to deal with the uncertainty of where we would settle in this large city of nearly 6 million people. We moved four times between June 1985 and September 1986. Our first HK apartment was on Peace Avenue, the second on Waterloo Road, the third on Victory Avenue, and the fourth on Canton Road. The first three apartments were provisions to us from YFC. We moved from Peace Avenue to Waterloo Road because the director sold that apartment. It was an extra apartment that he owned. We moved from Waterloo Road to Victory Avenue because YFC sold that property. We moved from Victory Avenue to our own apartment because that property was also put up for sale. We moved into our own apartment on Canton Road just prior to our second child's birth. We rented that apartment from September 1986 until the end of September 1987.

During August 1985, I made my first trip into Shenzhen, PRC. American couple named Mike and Jackie Cook went with me. HK was still a British Colony. By God's grace, we easily moved Chinese Bibles past the Communist customs guards. We dropped them at a predetermined location in Shenzhen. We spent a few hours in Shenzhen, and then, returned to HK the same day.

The Lord's calling on my life to preach the Gospel yielded amazing results. 28 souls professed faith in Christ during August. God used Mike Cook and me to preach the Gospel in many places and to many people. Glory to God!

We were surprised that the New Life Evangelistic Center in St. Louis sent us a donation of $200. They also published an article that I wrote entitled, "What's so Bad about Fear?"

> Fear hinders the flow of the Spirit. Many people are in fear's bondage. They feel an urge to love those around them, yet the same voice that convinced the priest and the Levite not to stop for the beaten traveler on the Jericho road convinces them not to get involved. Then, on top of their initial fear, a second fear sets in, "I should have helped the person I passed by." They have sinned! John

wrote, "There is no fear in love, but perfect love casts out fear, because fear has torment. He that fears is not made perfect in love." [9]

Many people live in fear of danger or rejection. God has made a way of escape. The way is to repent. "God gives grace to the humble." [10] The way of escape is to realize God's forgiveness (1 John 1:9); to believe in Jesus Christ (John 5:24); and to be renewed by the Holy Spirit (Titus 3:5-7). Christ lifts those who receive His Spirit of love, so that it can be said of them, "They overcame him (the devil) by the blood of the Lamb, and by the word of their testimony; and they loved not their lives unto death." [11]

We made our first family mission trip to Guangzhou City, PRC, on September 28, 1985. It was "Moon Festival" weekend. We left YFC at 1 pm. We saw our bus approaching the bus stop, but we were not quite there yet. Due to a time crunch, I started running to stop the bus. I did not want to wait for the next bus. Suddenly, Sherry fell and hit the sidewalk. Miraculously, Grace, who had been in her arms, was sitting on the sidewalk not scratched or crying. Sherry was on her hands and knees in pain. I picked up Grace and then helped Sherry up. Sherry could hardly stand on her own. Her knee was gouged open and bleeding. She had multiple scratches on her arms and hands. Onlookers asked,

---

[9] 1 John 4:18
[10] James 4:6
[11] Revelation 12:11

"Do you want us to call an ambulance?" We prayed. Sherry rested. We cleaned the wound and covered it with bandages. Sherry limped around during most of the trip due to the cut being directly on the bend of her knee.

When we reached the departure immigration booth, the officer told me that I did not have a HK re-entry visa in my passport. He said that if I left HK, I would lose my work permit status. I knew I had a re-entry visa, so we departed HK. Later, I found the re-entry visa in my passport.

After we settled down in our ship cabin, Grace started sneezing. Her nose was running. She felt feverish.

When we arrived at our destination, the gate was closed. No one in sight! We waited. Suddenly, an army truck pulled up. It was loaded with soldiers. We decided it was a good time to buy Grace water at a nearby market. Apparently, the soldiers were stationed nearby. We noticed that one soldier had a machine gun.

We finally met the pastors at the Dong Shan Church. We had scarcely started dialoguing when loud rapid bangs rang out. Grace was so scared that she just curled her lip. Held her breath! Tears rolled down her face. She could not make a sound to cry. The shots rang out again. Mr. Kao, the Vice-President of the Guangzhou Christian Council smiled and said, "It's the Moon Festival. People traditionally light firecrackers on this day." We had to call our meeting to an end because we could not hear each other over the louds pops of firecrackers.

By the time we reached our hotel, we were exhausted. Grace was warm with fever and congested. Ants crawled into bed with us and bit us from time to time. It was a difficult night. The Holy Spirit empowered us to thank God that we were counted worthy to suffer for Christ's name's sake.

In the PRC, we drank scalding hot water. This was to ensure that it had been boiled. The water had too many bacteria in it to drink it from the tap. When Grace saw a cup of water, she put her fingers into it to play with the water. She immediately pulled them out with tears. Later, I accidentally closed my briefcase on her fingers. Once again, she cried. Poor baby Grace!

The Lord provided blessings along the way. A Chinese woman offered to tell a taxi driver where to take us. She could understand English. We went to the Tung Fang Hotel. This was where our return train trip train tickets were being held for us. A Chinese man who spoke English helped us speak to the next taxi driver. A lady named Lo Yuen interpreted for us during our meetings at the church.

On Sunday, we attended the Dong Shan Church. It was a Three-Self Patriotic Movement (TSPM) congregation. The three principles they followed were self-governance, self-support, and self-propagation. These principles were first articulated by Henry Venn, General Secretary of the Church Missionary Society from 1841 to 1873. The principles were drafted formally during an 1892 conference in Shanghai of Christian missions. Dixon Edward Hoste, head of the China Inland Mission, was known for putting these principles into practice so that the Chinese would establish their own indigenous churches.

During the Sunday worship service, Pastor Cheng Po Chieh, Chairman of the Guangzhou TSPM committee, spoke from Philippians 1:1-6, Acts 1:12-14 and Acts 2:43-47. He emphasized unity for sake of propagating the Gospel. He differentiated between Christian unity and Moon Festival unity. Mrs. Lo Yuen told us she came to believe in Christ at this church.

We met for two-hours with Young-Chung Kao, Vice-president of the Guangzhou Christian Council and Manager over the Care Center project. My boss, David Chu, sent me to meet with these men. They were requesting financial support for a Care Center that they wanted to build. David wanted me to verify if it was a project worthy of support. They verified to me that chapel services and Bible studies would be a part of the Care Center's program. They told us of a Mr. Chueng who opened the first privately run hospital in Guangzhou. A Seventh Day Adventist Hospital! They wanted to do social services for the sake of improving the image of Christianity in the PRC. The Care Center was to be built on a piece of property that was 8,611 square feet in size. The land had the ruins of church on it. They planned to build a 4,305 square-foot building on it. They projected that the building would be 6-8 stories high. The cost to build back then was $11 per square-foot. The total projected cost of the building was $275,000. The first four floors were to house 160 elderly people with 20 rooms on each floor and two people in each room.

They planned to have a shower, a steam cooker, a wash basin, a toilet, two beds, two chairs, one desk, one dresser and one closet in each room. They planned to have a laundry room, elevator, kitchen, cafeteria, and chapel in the facility. They planned to have English and computer classes. They planned to offer medical services to children with hepatitis. They planned to offer accommodations for tourists and donors. They said that the Seventh Day Adventist Hospital would provide doctors and nurses for the Care Center.

We were told that local pastors were onboard with this project. They were seeking donations and interest-free loans. After the project was complete, they would depend on the pensions of the elderly to keep Care Center operational.

In response to their presentation, I recommended that they improve their English-language promotional literature; recruit an independent firm to verify their use of funds; and produce periodical progress reports. I assured them that I would share their vision with the YFC leadership in HK, which I did. My report was received by the YFC leadership, but I was not informed as to what they planned to do towards this project.

Did anything good come out of this trip? Yes, we got to share the Gospel with two men. One was a computer technician whose English name was John. John confessed a feeling of enslavement to the world. He was not satisfied with his life. He agreed with God's Word that our earthly lives are short. We urged

John to believe in Christ. He thanked us for sharing with him. He even paid for our meal without telling us.

Grace was free from fever and congestion by the time we returned to HK. I was allowed back into HK as a resident worker. Sherry and Grace received 30-day visitor visas.

Back in HK on November 3, after the Reachout Singers gave an altar call at an Assemblies of God Church, the Holy Spirit moved me to lay hands on three believers. They began to praise the Lord. They began speaking in tongues as the Spirit gave them utterance. We had prayed for 45-minutes prior to this meeting. God moved in ways above and beyond our expectation.

On December 8, the Lord empowered me to speak a large auditorium full of people. Ten people professed faith in Christ. Volunteers met with them afterwards to pray with them.

YFC did a rally with nearly 400 people in attendance. By God's grace, I preached a message on the curse of sin and on Christ the curse remover. God gave me two revelations. First, Adam and Eve's sin did not seem so bad. They only took a little fruit. The problem was that God told them not to do it. They disobeyed God. I asked the crowd, "How many of you disobey God at least once per day?" Everyone raised their hands. I told them that sin defiles us but Christ sanctifies us. Secondly, I told them that God used a shepherd boy named David and a fisherman named Peter to change the course of history and to change many people's lives. After the message, I prayed with new believers.

On December 19, The Carpenter's Tools sang at a large shopping mall. YFC workers distributed tracts to the crowd. I met a Jewish man named Daniel Ofri. He knew the Old Testament well. Evangelist Mike MacDonald and I invited Daniel out to eat. He listened to us for five hours as we shared about Jesus with him. Daniel's job was to get Jews to relocate to Israel. He led 250 Jews during 1985 to move to Israel. We prayed that Daniel would be compelled by the Holy Spirit to turn to Y'shua Ha Mashiach.

Due to illness, Sherry returned to the US with Grace. Sherry's mother kept this note that I wrote to Sherry, "You are extremely precious, loved and longed-for wife and daughter. I pray and think of you and Grace almost 24-hours a day, because even when I sleep, you're still on my mind. I believe that you and Grace will soon be here. Samson Chu received a word from the Lord that you would be back soon. God our Father is answering my prayers so quickly and abundantly. This morning, I was up at 3:30 am and reading the Bible. I'm on 2 Chronicles 26. The Lord's Word is increasing my faith and giving me joy. I hope that you are equally becoming stronger in the knowledge of His grace and goodness."

On December 25, after 59 days absence, Sherry and Grace returned from the US. What a wonderful gift from God! We appreciated those who prayed for us. Sherry told her parents, "Grace is thoroughly enjoying Mark. She jumps on him when he is lying down doing his work. He then plays with her. Grace calls him duggle-duggit and imitates his actions and words."

Sherry wrote to her parents, "We are presently staying in a five-room apartment owned by YFC. We are donating $200 per month to YFC for its use. We are bothered from time to time with ants and lizards, but not really suffering." Sherry did fine with navigating her way through airports during her return flight. She was just extremely exhausted.

On December 27 – 28, a church invited me to lead two Bible studies at their youth camp. Sherry and Grace joined me. A bright sun, blue sky, beautiful trees, green grass, tall mountains, and a trickling stream were our backdrop. I was happy that Sherry was with me. She had several good insights into the Scriptures for the young people. Sherry and I met at a Bible study, so it was good to be among the Chinese doing what we enjoy most. The young people thanked us for teaching them.

~ Chapter 3 ~
Called by the Gospel (1986)

During January 1986, Sherry delivered a message from the Lord to Filipina maids. The Lord directed Sherry through prayer to tell them about singing, praising and visible outward actions to lift their hearts out of depression. She shared with them how the Lord delivered her from anxiety, fear, and frustration by singing Psalms. The bottom line of her message was that faith in Son of God helps believers to press on.

During February, Sherry had a girl grab her arm after she handed her a Gospel tract. The girl wanted to hear more. All that we could share with her in Cantonese was, "Yehsou ngoi neih" and "Yehsou bei lei wihngsahng" (Jesus loves you) and (Jesus gives you eternal life). How our hearts yearned to tell her more! This incident impressed on us our need to learn Cantonese.

After prayer, we received the name of a language school. It was 40% less expensive than other schools. The cost for seven weeks of study, five days per week and three hours per day was $250. We asked God for the money for me to study. The money arrived just in time to enroll. Praise the Lord!

The Spirit of Christ compelled me to witness and to pray for people. For example, one day while walking home, I passed by a shop where men were gambling. The Holy Spirit brought Ezekiel 3:18 to my mind. It is the verse about God requiring the blood of wicked of us if He tells us to warn them, and we do not do it. The Lord challenged me to love these men enough to be

29

concerned for their eternal souls. I walked on but knew that the Lord wanted me to turn around. I did. I walked past the shop. This time in the opposite direction. The third time, I came to the shop, I entered in. They stopped gambling. I held out Bible tracts to them and said, "Seung bei lei tai" (I give you to read). They replied, "No!" I added, "Yehsou haih Jyu" (Jesus is Lord). My Cantonese was too limited to say more. I left but continued to pray for them. When I arrived home, Sherry was sick. I prayed for her. Later she told me, "I felt better after you prayed for me." Glory to God!

My second evangelism seminar was blessed with 19 trainees. My assistant instructors were Mira Hernando, Richard Ng, Lawrence Chui, and Ann Yu. We thanked God for them. Dwight L. Moody said, "It is better to win 10 to work than to do the work of 10." One trainee testified of three salvations after she shared the Gospel with them.

Last night, we enjoyed a fellowship meal with our four assistant instructors. We shared Scriptures and prayer concerns one with another. We also praised the Lord for the good results of the seminar.

Mira Hernando told us of Filipino pastors who work hard to earn $25 per month. They can barely afford to feed their family rice. I asked her to have the neediest pastors write me and send me their pictures. Mira's husband attended a seminary in the Philippines while she worked as a maid in HK. As a college science teacher in the Philippines, she earned $54 per month. As a maid in HK, she earned $290 a month. Mira hoped that someday I would teach evangelism and discipleship lessons to pastors in the Philippines. She was concerned that communism would take over the Philippines.

Mira asked us if we would help her start a fellowship for Filipina ladies. So, Sherry started by providing an invocation for the all-women church. I gave the first message. There were 15 people at the first meeting. The second week, 29 ladies attended. Two other missionaries offered to serve these ladies.

A middle-aged man came to Christ! As Lai Kit shared with him, I prayed, "Lord, if the devil can break a good man's will to resist evil, then, you can break an evil man's will to resist God." The Lord did the work. Billy Graham once said, "Mass crusades, in which I believe and to which I have committed my life, will never finish the Great Commission; but one-by-one ministry will." The man described above was saved by Christ while sitting in a public park. Glory to God!

The Lord made our long days fruitful and joyful. My days began with wake-up at 4:45 am, work at 6:00 am, with language studies, a 10-minute lunch break and a return to home by 6:00 pm. My weekends involved seminar preparation and teaching.

As the time neared for us to move out of YFC's Victory Avenue apartment, we looked diligently for an apartment that we could afford to rent. We could afford to pay $175 per month in rent and still make ends meet. Some options to rent that we looked at included: A rooftop apartment made of tin with no sink, toilet, shower, or kitchen. The rent there was $211 per month.

Another option was to rent one room and share public facilities with several families. The cost of one room was within our budget but offered no safety for Sherry and Grace while I was away. We looked at another apartment with ten rooms. Each of the rooms had an electricity meter. YFC offered to pay half the rent per month and use five of the rooms for their overseas guests who frequented HK. The rent was $550 per month. The owner was a Christian and wanted to rent to Christians.

A local government hospital agreed to help Sherry with delivering our second baby (Glory) at no charge. Sherry was due on September 30. She and the baby were in good health. Grace was sixteen months old.

After being sick for a while, Sherry was able to eat basic foods again. We appreciated the Americans who offered to send food to us. The Lord answered prayers prayed for our nutrition. A Chinese couple provided Kentucky Fried chicken for us. A couple invited us and seven other missionaries to a feast. A kind soul invited us to a meal at the Sheridan Hotel. Others brought us groceries on three separate occasions.

We made a ministry trip to the PRC on March 29 – 30. We planned the trip by faith that the Lord would supply our needs. I asked the Lord, "Is this Your will?" The Lord said to me, "You are well able to take the land." I thanked the Lord in advance. The next day, we received money in the mail to cover the cost. 40 pounds of Bibles were distributed. We dialogued with several people. They received our Gospel tracts.

The Bible and Literacy League located in Hillsboro, Missouri, gave Sandy Potenski and Sandy Watson our contact information. They came to visit us. We took them out to eat and told them of HK's need for missionaries. They assured us that they would pray about it.

Portuguese Jorge and British Sally approached us because of their interest to do mission work in HK. They had just finished four months of intensive service in Israel. I shared with them about YFC. They enjoyed doing Gospel tract ministry. They helped me assemble 100 evangelism workbooks. They made nine Bible courier trips to the PRC. Revival Christian Ministries International (RCMI) decided to sponsor their visas so they could do evangelism. They were zealous witnesses for Christ.

I met a British lady named Ann Britton at the language school. She was an older woman with grown children. I told her of YFC's need for someone to compose, edit, and send letters to supporters who speak English. She decided to volunteer with YFC three-days per week.

During May, we were blessed to teach an evangelism seminar to 170 Filipina ladies. Five trainees helped me to teach the seminar. Sherry shared her salvation testimony and three ladies believed in Christ for the first time. One lady handed us a letter with the following testimony:

Dear beloved brother and sister in Christ Jesus, Czanderna Family! Praise the Lord, grace be unto you and peace from

God our Father and from the Lord Jesus Christ. I thank my God always on your behalf, for the grace of God which is given for you and for me by Jesus Christ. Your desire to prove faithful and serve Him has greatly encouraged and blessed me. May He bless you for that and I pray that the Spirit of God anoint you in a special way throughout your life for His own glory. In Jesus' Name. Amen. As a reciprocating factor, please pray for me also to seek God's will in my life. Thank you very much about the sharing and the boldness to evangelize. Sister in Christ, Elma Labrador.

The sponsoring Church wrote us the following letter:

Thank you very much for being willing to come and help us with the subject of evangelism. We appreciate all the time, prayer, and preparation you put into your very good presentations We praise the Lord for providing you all to assist us in this valuable training.

Trainees testified of nine new believers from their Gospel sharing efforts. God is good! Praise the Lord!

YFC hosted an evangelism seminar in Cantonese using the booklet I helped to produce. At the end of the seminar, 34 trainees committed themselves to do evangelism for the next year. Two more churches, a seminary and a Christian fellowship requested YFC to provide seminars at their locations.

I spoke to young adults at Revival Christian Church (RCC) via an interpreter. They were eager to hear God's Word. I spoke to them about undergoing labor pains for lost souls prior to experiencing the joy of spiritual parenthood. I showed them how to use paper folding methods to illustrate Gospel truths.

I learned something about those who worship Buddha from one of my English language students. She told me that those who worship Buddha never speak of their troubles to him. They only hope that their problems will be resolved.

Grace experienced a long season of good health. She grew in wisdom, strength, and stature. Her favorite word for everything was "Bible." She tried to vacuum and hang clothes to help Sherry with the household chores. We asked people to pray for her appetite to increase. We asked people to pray for Sherry's prenatal visits. Communication at the hospital was difficult.

"This week, 81-year-old Doug Fraser sent us a check for $35. His closing remark was, "Go buy some lunch for your family with this." His envelope only had a $0.22 stamp on it. This was insufficient postage to send a letter from the US to HK. God answered a prayer that I prayed that He would bring us money on the backs of angels. I was surprised that an elderly man from Chicago was God's chosen weapon to give us a victory over food deficiency. Glory to God!

Mike Adkins sang a beautiful song in schools and churches this month based on Psalm 105:43-45: "He [the Lord] brought out His people with joy, His chosen ones with gladness.

He gave them the lands of the Gentiles, and they inherited the labor of the nations, that they might observe His statutes and keep His laws. Praise the Lord!" [12] We have adopted this song as our anthem of confidence in the Lord.

The Lord put it on Sherry and my heart to distribute Gospel tracts. Last December, the HK Bible Society supplied us with 3,000 tracts. We used these tracts to initiate conversations with people about Jesus.

On Wednesday, May 6, Eddie Tamm, and I shared the Gospel with a 74-year-old man who believed in Christ. We had two follow-up meetings with him. He was nearly blind. He depended on the kindness of a friend who provided a room and two meals per day for him.

Sherry taught Elsa, Maggie, Rebecca, and Terry how to speak English (free of charge). The lessons lasted 1-2 hours each week. She taught them English from Grace's picture Bible. She had them explain the pictures in their best possible English. This forced them to speak English. They also confessed Scripture as they explained the pictures. They were grateful for Sherry's help. Rebecca Ho and Terry were Christians. Elsa and Maggie had not yet believed in or professed Christ as their Lord.

Two weeks ago, Louise wrote these words to us, "I am praying that God will open the windows of heaven and pour down blessings on you to meet all your needs." Last week, we met eight

---

[12] Psalm 105:43-45 NKJV

Americans. We helped them with their short-term mission in HK. Before they left for the airport, they gave us three boxes of American food. The kind that we could not afford. They also bought us clothing and gave us $120 in cash. God answered Louise's prayer. During their time with us, they loved us with the love of the Lord. They refreshed us with a wonderful sense of being valuable to God and to others.

During June, I had the privilege to share the Gospel with 12 boys at a juvenile detention center. One of them believed in Christ. I gave them Bibles. The guard said that they would likely read the Bibles through many times since they had little else to do. Praise the Lord!

By God's grace, we delivered 30 pounds of Bibles to believers in the PRC. Guards detained the man ahead of me and asked him to open his luggage. I prayed, "Lord, if the devil can blind so many Christians to the needs of the lost, then, please blind this lost person to what Your Christian is trying to do," The guard waved me through.

Mark Albrecht and I moved 200 pounds of Bibles between the two of us. Our team members did not show up. Thanks to the grace of God, the Bibles reached their destination.

We were not able to rent an apartment for our family due to insufficient income, so we decided to make a return trip to the US from June 19 – July 28. Our return airline tickets were about to expire. The purpose of our trip was to increase our monthly ministry support. Thankfully, several pastors invited us to share with their congregations about our mission work.

KNLC, Channel 24's president, Larry Rice, interviewed us on TV during our visit to the US. The listening audience called in and asked us questions. A man named Joe told us that he wanted to be saved, so I led him to pray to Jesus. Joy filled our hearts!

Last night, Ozark Airline closed the baggage claim area before we got our luggage. We had to wait until the morning to get our suitcases. After that, we made our way to the South Shore Station and boarded a train to Michigan City. My Mom picked us up at 10:15 am. Thankfully, the Lord provided for us four venues where we could share about our mission.

After returning to HK, I wrote a letter to Sherry's parents and siblings:

> Thank you for being so kind to us. You fed, housed, clothed, transported us, and helped us care for Grace while we were there. You booked meetings for us. You talked to your Christian friends on our behalf. You let us use your telephone. You sent out invitations for our meetings. You studied the Bible and prayed with us. You made us feel thoroughly loved. We are really blessed to have such a family as you all.

In the last newsletter, we asked for prayer that God would provide for me three to seven Chinese to help me do Bible tract ministry and that YFC would allow me more time to do this kind of ministry. God answered prayer. YFC allotted to me three days per week, two-hours each day for evangelism ministry. The Lord supplied interpreters for me. Over 1,000 Gospel tracts were distributed last week. These tracts helped me to initiate Gospel conversations with more than 30 people. Praise the Lord!

We noticed people setting trays of food on the sidewalks and burning incense sticks near those trays. I asked Samson Chu what the meaning of this was. He said, "They believe that the gates of hell are open and that dead spirits are wandering around. The people are afraid that if they don't set a gift out for the ghosts, that the ghosts will attack and curse them." August 23 – 25 are the actual dates of the "Ghost Festival" for those who observe these practices.

During September, we did Gospel tract distribution in public places three times per week. Nine souls were saved by Christ during the last ten days. Many others heard the Gospel. One convert, Cheng Yu Man started attending Church. YFC interns Simon, Lisa and Winner took turns helping me evangelize. They also helped me follow-up with the new believers.

Sharing the Gospel with strangers required divine power. Apart from the Lord, I could not do it. Before an outreach, I was oppressed with fears and doubts. Then, God would remind me that it was not my love – but His! Not my strength – but His! Not my faith – but His faithfulness! Only God could open the eyes of the blind. No one can come to the Jesus apart from the Father. [13] We urged our intercessors to ask the Father for converts.

Before sinners repented, I claimed Bible promises for them. For example, "Where sin abounded, grace abounded exceedingly more…" [14] "The opening of Thy Word gives light, it imparts understanding to the simple." [15]

Sherry sang at a church in To Ko Wan. Two people there professed faith in Christ for the first time. She sang at Methodist Church on Victoria Island and at a seminar. The Lord used her willingness sing in front of people to open doors of ministry.

Sherry's sister Louise came to help us prior to our daughter Glory's birth. She arrived in HK on September 3. During that time, YFC asked Louise to share God's Word with young people at a Christian camp. One of the girls that Louise contacted had the English name Happy. Happy started visiting our home and bringing friends with her. They enjoyed playing with Grace and Glory. Happy eventually became a believer in Christ and a teacher at a Pentecostal primary school. Louise also shared God's Word with Filipina maids at three different venues. Glory to God!

Cheng Yu Man, one of the converts from last week, had no home. After we prayed and made phone calls, the Lord connected me with Youth with a Mission. They took Yu Man in. They operated a shelter and a feeding ministry.

---

[13] John 6:65
[14] Romans 5:20
[15] Psalm 119:130

25 trainees and leaders from six different fellowships attended our evangelism seminar on September 14. The leaders asked us to teach the seminar in their churches. David Chu taught this seminar as a 24-hour accredited course at the HK China Bible Seminary between September 9 – November 11.

Louise, Sherry, and I, along with a short-term missionary couple named Mike and Pam MacDonald shared at six high schools and two churches between October 31 – December 1. Some of the assemblies involved more than 500 students. Louise and Sherry sang. I preached and gave altar calls. Mike shared his testimony. Pam did worship songs with choreographed motions.

Louise wrote down her observations about HK:

The Lord says in Romans 1 that where there is idolatry, there is also a spiraling degradation of human lives into gross perverted sinfulness. Yesterday, we saw a man sleeping on the sidewalk. He was the dirtiest person I've ever seen. Dirt was matted and encrusted on his unwashed body. It was so saddening, because the man must not value even the tiniest worth of his life and soul. The sidewalk had a wet mixture of smashed rotting food, blood from butchered animals and countless fish scales on it. I have seen at least 30 men like this man in one week.

However, the warmth and the welcome of Christians here and their faith in Christ are unlike any other. They have a contagious life penetrating love for Jesus and, an affection for the saints and a loving burden for the lost.

Almost every day or night, Sherry experiences pangs but then they stop. During August, we switched from planning the baby to be born at the government free Kowloon Hospital to the Baptist Hospital. The conditions at the free hospital are deplorable, plus, almost no one speaks English there which makes communication between the staff and us nearly impossible. Please believe with us for a healthy delivery and for Sherry and the baby to be well.

"The baby is coming!" Sherry gasped. The call button was on, but no one came. The Lord moved me to run to the nurses' station for help. At 10:22 pm (9:22 am CST), on October 1, Glory Christina was born. The Lord used a nurse to deliver Glory. She weighed six pounds and thirteen ounces. She was healthy as was Sherry. Praise the Lord! God answered prayer.

Remember Fred Phelps from a previous newsletter? Fred visited HK again this month. This time he had good news. He believed in Christ. Praise the Lord!

A Filipina named Rebecca also shared her testimony with us this month. She said that her life changed after I shared the Gospel with her last year. She became a women's fellowship leader. Praise the Lord!

33-year-old Lau Chi Yi lost hope to keep living. He quit his job and considered suicide. His brother, Alan Lau, introduced him to us after hearing my salvation testimony at a meeting. On

October 8, Chi Yi believed in Christ. Alan's family of three went to church with us this month. The Lau family introduced us to their relatives as well. This entire family and their relatives were a result of Sherry's teaching English to a Chinese girl named Terry.

Sherry's sister, Louise, read a book by Jackie Pullinger entitled, "Chasing the Dragon." She shared the following stories from this book with us:

> Prostitutes raise babies that are given to them until the girls are nine years old, then, begin to use them in porn films and porn magazines to earn money for them. They also rent them out to men for sexual use. Hundreds of prostitution signs decorate both sides of the streets near our apartment. Jackie Pullinger is assigning some of her converts to do late night witnessing with me. Through Christ and the baptism of the Holy Spirit, prostitutes have been transformed into zealous Christians.

Louise led a Bible study for young people. On Saturdays, she did a Bible study with Happy, Pui Man, Pui Yi, Pui Sze and Yeuk Hong in our apartment. These girls helped to get Louise invited to speak at their school. She spoke to a group of 50 students and their parents. They gave Louise 90-minutes to share.

Sherry sang for a large audience at the huge China Fleet Club on November 2. This was where the Filipina Fellowship of the International Christian Assembly met on Sundays. We did a seminar there for Filipinas on love, courtship, and marriage. The theme of our sharing was "Compatibility through the Holy Spirit."

YFC's Lisa, Winner and Simon did personal evangelism with me six days per week. 20 professed faith in Christ during October. These converts included three small boys, two 15-year-old boys, a 44-year-old woman, a 52-year-old man and a 78-year-old man. Glory to God!

This month, I had a 68-year-old Australian named Aleck for a travelling companion. We took four heavy bags of Bibles into the PRC. We went nearly 24-hours without eating due to our tight schedule. Aleck was diabetic. I prayed that the Lord would provide food for him. Once our Bibles were distributed, we returned to the border to purchase eight entry visas for eight passports. These passports belonged to other Bible couriers. The big blessing here was that the passport officer offered Aleck a full breakfast. She shared with us about her life. She graduated from high school last year. She was contracted to serve two years as a passport inspector. She lived in a dormitory. Her family lived 120 miles from her. She saved her four-days off per month until the end of the month so that she could travel to see them.

During November, Janny Fong told us, "My father reads people's faces." HK had diviners. Janny asked us to pray for him. We did. We also asked an all-night prayer group to pray for him. A week before his conversion, Janny threw out her family's idols. On November 8, we shared the Gospel with Mr. Fong and invited him to attend Paul Yonggi Cho's crusade with us. On November

9, Janny's sister believed in Jesus. On November 12, her father believed in Christ. Great joy filled Janny's heart and ours. On November 18, we had our first follow-up meeting with Mr. Fong. He professed love for Jesus.

The Lord led me to share with various people. Gangsters in doorways! Old men gambling on a sidewalk! A teenage prostitute vomiting on the street! Boys sitting on the curbside staring at pornography! Souls in bondage to Satan! Most of them were between the ages of 12-25. Satan hated them and wanted them left alone, but greater was He who was in us than he who was in the world. [16]

There are about 4,000 street sleepers at night. Some are mentally ill. All are poor. "Jesus, please set them free from Satan." The Psalmist wrote, "All my bones shall say, 'Lord, who is like You, delivering the poor from him who is too strong for him, yes, the poor and the needy from him who plunders him?'" [17]

Sherry sang at three meetings this month. 7 out of 40 believed in Christ at a Baptist High School. 35 came forward for salvation at the International Christian Assembly. Teresa Tchino was the first woman I prayed with. She confessed Christ with tears streaming down her face. Another committed herself to seek a Christian education and serve God. Three elderly people confessed Christ at a Pentecostal Church. We also assisted Mike and Pam MacDonald with outreaches. The Reach Out Singers

---

[16] 1 John 4:18
[17] Psalm 35:10

from South Dakota and local YFC teams did programs in schools and churches as well. Many salvations were reported. 1,542 students attended five high school meetings led by our YFC teams. 34 conversions were recorded at the three high schools.

Mike MacDonald and I witnessed to people in a fortune telling district. He spotted some British people having their palms read. He said to them, "Every time you look at the palms of your hands from now on, I want you to remember that Jesus' palms were nailed to a tree for your sins."

Sherry's sister Louise made two trips to the PRC this month with missionary Pearl Corbin. During the first trip, they shared the Gospel with a 25-year-old named Shan. During the second trip, they shared the Gospel with Shan's brother and friend. Louise had prayed that she would have the opportunity to share the Gospel inside the PRC. God answered her prayer.

Louise returned to the US on November 17. She left behind a group of teens for Sherry to disciple. Sherry continued to do Saturday morning Bible studies with them. Her interpreter was Virginia Kam. The disciples were Happy, Pui Man, Pui Yi, Pui Sze, Yeuk Hong, Chiang Wai, and Pak Ai.

After Louise returned to America, we shared our small 350 square foot nest with various guests. One very special guest and blessing to our family was Anne Hepburn from New Zealand. Anne started the Dayspring Bookstore in HK.

Two healing miracles took place in our family. First, Grace's arm pulled out of place causing her severe pain. Sherry prayed for Grace, and she was healed. I had a 101-degree fever and stomach cramps but worked five hours and afterwards climbed to the top of a small mountain where there was a Buddhist temple. Mike MacDonald and I witnessed to the people there. After that, I attended a birthday party until 10 that evening. I woke up the next morning healed. The Lord also healed many sick people at the Yonggi Cho crusade this week.

The Lord provided resources for me to take another seven weeks of Cantonese lessons. I thank God for Sherry's father. He sent the extra money I needed to enroll in these classes.

We gave the following names to our prayer partners to pray for: Ko Sze To a teacher from the PRC receptive to the Gospel; Robert Fong a new believer; Yuen Yee and Pui Hung ages ten and eight respectively; Alex Lee interested in Jesus; Ah Wing Sang attended a follow-up session after believing in Christ; Kong Kwok professed faith; Kai Lung and Ka Kin listened to the Gospel but did not believe; Lee Piu received and studied the Bible with us; Leung Hei a 77-year old who recently lost her husband and two sons; Wan Hi received and studied Bible with us; Cheng Shing enjoyed listening to Bible teaching; Siu Yin and Yok Li two teenage girls who were open to the Gospel; Yin Lan whom I showed where to attend church; and, Wong Wing and Kam Kiu who received and studied the Bible with us. The Lau family listened to the Gospel, attended church, went through spiritual counseling, and came to our apartment to hear more about Jesus. Fu Gwai was a police officer who listened to the Gospel. His

47

mother was a devoted Christian. He attended a policeman's fellowship. Sherry taught Maggie Siu English lessons from Christian magazines. Louise took her to a Woman's Aglow meeting and to hear Yonggi Cho at the crusade. Sherry taught Wai La English and shared the Gospel with her. She was in her 20's. Mrs. Lai, the mother of Elaine Lai, who worked at YFC, wanted to know why God allowed suffering. Her husband left her years ago. We asked our intercessors to pray for them.

On November 20, Mr. Leroy Biesenthal of the Lutheran Church Missouri-Synod invited us out for lunch. He cared for lost souls and for the follow-up of new believers, Mr. Biesenthal arranged for me to speak at the Lutheran Seminary on the topic of evangelism. I took my students out to do personal evangelism.

December 15 – 17, I prayed earnestly for the Lord Jesus to defend our ministry. Satan moved people to oppose our Gospel sharing ministry in public places. On December 18, a Chinese co-worker, full of joy, showed me an article from a magazine with worldwide circulation, entitled, "Chinese Around the World." The article was a prayer request that I had submitted to YFC to ask their prayer supporters to pray for us. The article was about the 96% of HK people who still need Jesus. That same day, Glory Wong called and said she wanted to help me reach lost souls. May the Good News of God's great love always flow freely to souls who are ready to receive it!

~ Chapter 4 ~
Called by the Gospel (1987)

On New Year's Day, by God's grace and provision, Tom
Collins and I contacted four boys ages 15 – 20. We shared the
Gospel with them for an hour. Tom prayed for me, and the Holy
Spirit anointed my ability to understand and speak Cantonese. I
kept asking the boys, "Do you understand what I am saying?"
They replied, "Understand" each time. The 20-year-old boy, Ah
Chen, prayed to Jesus. This happened in Shenzhen.

Later in January, Sherry, Grace, Glory, and I met seven
women in Shenzhen, China. They gave us their addresses. We
met a man named Shan. He gave us his address. This meant that
we now had 12 addresses of people in the PRC.

Back in HK, Ken Keung was concerned that gangsters
would find him. They had been harassing him. Simon and I asked
him for 10 minutes of his time to share the Gospel with him. We
stopped when the 10 minutes ended, but he asked us to keep
sharing. He believed in Jesus after hearing the Gospel message for
an hour. Glory to God!

Lai Sing was spiritually oppressed. Two Youth with a
Mission (YWAM) missionaries joined Simon and me to rebuke
the oppressive spirit out of the man in the Name of Jesus. Ah Sing
passed out. We laid him down on the sidewalk. When he revived,
I asked him, "Do you want to believe in Jesus?" He said, "Yes."
He professed Christ as his Savior – glory to God!

The Lord opened a door for me to preach at two different boy's schools with a combined population of 500 boys between the ages of 15 – 16. 38 of these boys professed faith in Jesus. They prayed the sinner's prayer. Praise the Lord!

The Lord blessed us with furniture for our apartment, including a double bed with large headboard; a wardrobe closet; a table for six people; benches with enough seating space for six; and a fan. YFC said that we could keep the refrigerator that they loaned us. The double-bed was beautiful. We used wood that contractors left behind to build cribs for Grace and Glory.

Numerous volunteers from RCC and myself did open air preaching in crowded areas of Mongkok. We distributed Gospel tracts to by-standers. People listened. RCC baptized more than 40 people during the last three months. Their auditorium was packed on Sundays.

One of the Shenzhen ladies mentioned earlier professed faith in Christ. Ruth and Matthew, Christians from HK, shared the Gospel with her. This was God's first convert via our Gospel sharing effort in the PRC. Praise the Lord!

On February 5, I met Kai Ho (Edward) in a park while distributing tracts. Edward professed faith in Christ. He said, "My sister is a Christian who prays for me to believe in Christ." On February 8, he attended church. On February 17, Edward brought his friend Tony along. Using an illustrated Gospel booklet and tract published by Jack Chick, the Lord helped me to tell them of the benefits of trusting in God. On February 18, Tony professed faith in Christ. On February 20, they had their first follow-up lesson. They were ages 15 – 16.

The Filipina trainees from previous evangelism seminars reported to us on January 28 that they had a total of 26 converts from their evangelistic efforts. One Filipina named Elma Labrador gave us $25.40 as a sacrificial gift to our mission. This offering replaced the last of our money which I had used to produce more evangelism booklets. Elma Labrador also attended our Follow-up Seminar wrote to us afterwards and said:

> Really, from four meetings on how to follow-up – I really am blessed because from the first meeting in our seminar, I started doing the methods for the lost souls, and for those who are newly born Christians – I mean to become mature. Brother and Sister, I'm glad to testify that with the help of the Holy Spirit there was a tremendous response regarding my follow-up.

The Lutheran Seminary asked me to do a 75-minute talk on March 4 about the ministries of Youth for Christ. I emphasized our Gospel preaching effort. Praise God!

A HK convert named Cheng Yu Man completed seven follow-up lessons. This was a miracle! Most people were slow to sacrifice their time and effort for God, but he was eager.

On February 14, Sherry laid hands on and prayed for the teens in our home Bible study group. Miew Tsang liked to listen to the testimony of believers. Happy wanted to see the Lord as we did. Song Yin and Pui Man were interested in miracles. Pak Kai was silent. Pui Szi, Pui Yi and Mei Yok returned to us after being absent for a while. We loved these teens.

Three students (ages 17 – 18) believed in Christ at a Pentecostal High School where I preached the Gospel. The Holy Spirit's anointing made the difference. Glory to God!

YFC asked me to challenge English speaking churches to receive the ministry of evangelist Jerry Powell. I called a Baptist pastor several times about a booking for February 15. The pastor never responded. The Spirit of God moved me to pray fervently for that pastor and within the same hour he called me to invite Jerry to speak. I trusted God to cause another church to respond. Two weeks passed. The same day that I thanked God for the victory, they called me and booked Jerry to speak on February 15. 50 Filipinas believed in Christ at the first meeting and 10 Filipinas believed in Christ at the second meeting. Praise the Lord. Nothing is impossible with God.

We scheduled a meeting in the PRC with Shan. He did not arrive. We prayed, "Lord, it cost us more than $30 for this trip. We are available. There are lost souls around us." We went out from the meeting place and found 10 children playing. The children were attracted to Grace and Glory. We shared Gospel tracts with them and urged them to pray to Jesus. A soldier appeared. We disappeared. We met several more children. I said to Sherry, "We can be detained for proselytizing people." She replied, "What about their souls?" Then, I remembered how Peter and John were ordered not to teach in the Name of Jesus, but the

Lord told them, "Tell the people the full message of this new life." [18] I approached an eight-year-old boy. I gave him a Gospel tract. Other children came running. Adults drew near. Then, the former group of 10 children returned. Using large pictures, I told them of the death, judgment, sin, damnation, Christ, faith, and eternal life. They repeated my Chinese words and sometimes corrected my pronunciation. They were standing on their toes like baby birds straining to reach food. We urged them to repent, pray to Jesus and receive His love. They thanked us.

Edward and Tony continued their follow-up lessons 1 – 2 times per week. They were punctual. They were attentive. I praised God for these disciples.

While evangelizing in HK, I met a woman from the PRC who had never heard about Jesus. I was the first one to share the Gospel with her. I experienced great joy!

The Lord provided a Christian dentist to extract three of Sherry's wisdom teeth for less than $35.00. He also gave us 15 cans of infant formula and many packets of baby cereal. God's grace and love are amazing!

During the 11-month financial period between 1986 – 1987, our total income, including money received as birthday gifts, was $12,402. Our ministry related expenses were $3,104. Our personal expenses were $9,298. Under ministry expenses, we used $2,027 on travel including a round-trip to the US to raise

---

[18] Acts 5:20, 28

support as well as to make 15 roundtrips to the PRC. We spent $400 to produce and to send our monthly newsletter to prayer partners. We spent $386 on Cantonese classes for me.

During April, the Saturday Bible Study group translated a Gospel tract from Chinese into English for Sherry. She challenged them to believe in Christ. Siu Ying boldly declared, "I believe in Jesus." Sherry said, "This means that you must follow Jesus only, keep His promises and repent of things that do not agree with His Word. Will you do this willingly?" "Yes!" he replied. Jo Ann from RCC interpreted the conversation. Siu Ying thanked the Lord for eternal life. We asked our prayer supporters to pray for Happy, Pak Kai, Pui Man, Miew Tsang, Yeuk Hong, Song Yee, Hon Fai, Hon Kau, Siu Ying, Cindy, and Catherine.

The 82-year-old mother of Mrs. Lam professed faith in Christ and was baptized. She received two months leave from the PRC to visit HK. The evening before she returned to the PRC, I prayed for her. As I did, she jumped and began to speak. Luther told me that as I was praying for her, she felt a warm sensation come over her and she experienced the peace of God. Praise God!

Mormons visited converts Edward and the Lam family. Mormons were active in HK. Thankfully, Edward and the Lam family were not led astray by them.

New believers this month included: Man Ho (16 years old), Mr. Cheung (29 years old), and Mrs. Wong, a woman with two sons that was recently raped by her landlord.

Sherry and three other missionary women taught English on Tuesday nights. One student said that he had never heard about the death and resurrection of Jesus Christ. I also taught a 17-year-old unbeliever English and shared the Gospel with him.

I preached my first message in Cantonese at a local church. I had the congregation read the Bible verses aloud in unison. I explained the verses as the Lord led me to do. Praise God! I began my last seven-week Cantonese course on April 28.

Anne Hepburn from New Zealand came to stay with us on April 1. Anne has served the Lord in many countries. Anne opened the Dayspring Christian Bookstore in HK.

We taught a leadership seminar in our apartment to five Filipina maids on May 3. These five ladies started a weekly worship service for Filipinas. Their goal was to ensure that their contacts professed faith in Christ and served Him.

A church asked me to speak on the spot. I was fatigued and sick. What did I do? I trusted the Lord to help me. The Holy Spirit gave me verse after verse from the Bible to share. He gave me illustrations to share. Five out of eleven newcomers professed faith in Christ for the first time. Praise God for His amazing grace.

Edward interpreted for me during two evangelistic outreaches. Two young people professed faith in Christ. Edward invited his friend Cecil to a meeting where I was sharing the Gospel. Cecil professed faith in Christ. Our joy was great. But after this, Edward's Buddhist parents forbade him to attend church anymore. We prayed for Edward.

During June, the Lord blessed with me an amazing opportunity to share the Gospel in Shenzhen. I shared the Gospel while standing in the front yard of a small sewing factory. So, many neighbors joined the meeting that there was no room left between the buildings. One man climbed up on the roof of a house to listen. The Lord anointed my voice to speak Cantonese understandably. Four people professed faith in Jesus. Later, I returned to the same factory to share the Gospel. This time, I brought 24 x 12-inch Bible picture cards with me. These picture cards were from the Accelerated Christian Education (A.C.E.) School of Tomorrow. They were a part of the curriculum that we used to teach Grace. I shared with the people about the life, death, resurrection, ascension, and present reign of Christ. I distributed 10 Chinese Bibles. Praise God for the spreading of His Word!

The miracle of today's event was that yesterday I had a fever of 101.4. I was achy, dizzy, and feeling totally depleted. At about nine the previous night, I called out to Jesus for our daughter Grace and myself. I begged the Lord for mercy. I had sung praise songs with Grace most of the evening. The devil told me, "Jesus doesn't want to hear your prayers." Suddenly, the Holy Spirit destroyed this lie by assuring me that Jesus had heard my prayer. I was instantly healed. Grace's fever went down. The Lord healed her of a sickness that had plagued her for three weeks. After I received my healing, I prepared my notes for sharing the Gospel in Cantonese.

I woke up at 6 am to reach the factory on time. It took me two-hours to cross the crowded border. It was muggy and hot. People smoked, drank beer, and rudely pushed and shoved. Cigarette smoke was in my face. After I crossed the border into the PRC, I boarded an overcrowded minibus. People stuck to one another due to excessive perspiration. The open bus windows were our only source of fresh air. The air flow stopped when the bus stopped. I had to pass through two security checkpoints to reach my destination. The area was surrounded by an electric fence. God got me past two security check points. The crowd around me blocked the guards from seeing me. Miracles can come in strange wrappings.

Another miracle was that Edward Kai Ho was baptized. He did not mind that I could not attend his baptism. He did not want me to cancel my trip to Shenzhen. Though the Holy Spirit used me to lead Edward to Jesus, and though his parents opposed his baptism, Edward went forward with his public profession of Christ as his Savior and Lord.

During July, six more factory workers in Shenzhen professed faith in Christ. This made a total of 10 new believers at this factory. Sherry sang to them two Chinese songs and I shared with them Scriptures. Sherry had twisted her ankle the night before the trip. The Lord healed her. She did six hours of traveling on her ankle painlessly. We were waved through a total of four security checkpoints. At one point, everybody was asked to get off the bus and to walk through inspection lines, but the bus attendant, saw our two babies, and motioned for us to stay on the bus. Praise the Lord!

One night, I prayed at Temple Street Park for an hour before reaching out to the people. I prayed, "Lord, please save this one from hell and that one too, etc." Eight people repented out loud that night and professed faith in Christ. Praise the Lord!

Between June 29 – July 2, a professional Gospel singing group from the US named Arise Unlimited sang at two churches inside the PRC. A Mr. Wan from the Heman Music School arranged the meetings. Before the meetings, government officials invited Mr. Wan and me to a meal. China's ambassador to Africa, the chief of police of Dong Guan and Tai Ping, and a few other high officials ate with us. I was concerned that my identity as a missionary would become known to these officials. Then, Psalm 23:5 came to mind, "You prepare a table for me in the presence of my enemies; You anoint my head with oil; my cup runs over." At that moment, the Holy Spirit gave me the sensation of oil running over my head. A love for these officials replaced my fear of them. During the meal, the officials spoke of cults from the US entering the PRC. By God's grace, I told them that many true believers in the US love and pray for the Chinese. They smiled.

During the first meeting, a Dong Guan television crew recorded the performance. The church was packed. It was sweltering hot and muggy. At 10:30 pm, the city's officials invited the team to perform on the 11th floor of our hotel where there was a discotheque. The members of Arise Unlimited sang and shared testimonies while disco lights flashed. Arise Unlimited sang in a second discotheque the next night.

At the second church meeting, due to lack of space, people stood outside the windows and doorways looking in. I shared my personal testimony, and the Gospel in Cantonese. Mr. Wan interpreted my Cantonese into English for the American team members, so I knew that the Holy Spirit had anointed my speech. After the meeting, two more people professed faith in Jesus.

The city's officials brought us bushel baskets full of lychee berries. More than we could eat! Lychees were expensive. The chief of police accompanied us on the bus during our two-hour trip back to the border. He was concerned for us because the bus driver had previously drove as fast as 66 miles per hour on dangerous roads. He passed by trucks on hills and curves. Most of us were terrified.

As we departed, the chief of police said to the team, "I am speechless. I am happy. Please come back and visit again. Please tell your American friends that we love them." The entire trip seemed like a dream. Many amazing things happened!

Back in HK, Edward Chan shared his written salvation testimony with me. He wrote, "I believed in God when I was 15. One day, I met Mr. Mark Czanderna in a park near my home. He preached to me Christ. Afterwards, I gave my phone number to him and became his friend. After I believed in God for three months, I was baptized at Revival Christian Church. I go to Mr. Mark's office to study about Christ. He helps me with my homework. I also help Mr. Mark preach in parks. Now, I study hard at school. I know that this has been God's help to me."

Recently, Richard and Martha Schaffer from Ashland, MO, recruited two young people from their church to write Happy and Miew Tsang. Louise wrote to them as well. This was an excellent way to encourage the new believers.

Amidst my records of our ministry, one letter listed names and ages of 24 Chinese people who I asked people to pray for. These were souls that Christ died for. Most were teenagers, but some were elderly. The average age of the 24 people was 21. YFC recorded 293 professions of faith in Christ during June and July. One young girl that we asked people to pray decided not to abort her unborn child. Her name was Pu Cho.

The Lord blessed the teaching and outreach at the Lutheran Seminary. We connected with poor people who lived just outside the seminary. Most of them lived in two-room apartments with about 120 square feet of floor space. They shared a public toilet and a public shower facility. They appreciated us. We had more outreaches planned for August 7, 14, 21, and 28.

In May, missionary Kevin Carrell stayed with us. When I told him of my heart to reach the people in the PRC, he urged me to apply to teach at Zhongshan University. I did. The university offered me free accommodations, plus monthly pay of $175. The one glitch to this offer was that the director stated that he did not need my services until the fall of 1988.

Setbacks at key moments tempted me to leave the mission field, but the Lord was faithful to encourage me. For example, on July 8, while at a prayer breakfast, the speaker said that once John Wesley was delayed due to a broken wagon wheel. While fixing the wheel, he met a farmer who was about to lose all his possessions to a creditor just because he could not pay a small sum of money. Wesley paid the farmer's debt, and his family was spared from losing everything. God had a purpose for our setback.

As I waited on the Lord, I envisioned receiving a letter. I believed in accordance with Amos 3:7 that God would show me if He was going to move us into the PRC. I meditated on, "The steps of a good man are ordered by the Lord, and He delights in his way. Though he falls, he shall not be utterly cast down; for the Lord upholds him with His hand." [19] Then, on July 27, I received a letter of acceptance from Zhongshan University. Praise God!

Zhongshan University was founded by a Christian named Dr. Sun Yatsun. It had a chapel on the campus from the days when Christianity was allowed. It was a beautiful place to be.

One evening before we moved to the PRC, 150 Christians gathered at Temple Street Park in HK for an outreach. Seven churches, three Christian ministries and many Christians sang and testified. This happened in front of a Guan Yin Temple.

I was sick with flu but thought I would join the outreach for at least 15-minutes to show my support. When I arrived at the

---

[19] Psalm 37:23-24

park, I felt severely depleted. I sat down on a park bench next to a drunk. The drunk wanted me to take him to a hospital in hope that with my advocacy they would admit him. I suggested that we pray to Jesus. He said to me, "I do not believe anything you are saying." He told me that he would pray to idols. He was so stubborn that I walked away from him. He got up and followed me. He proclaimed, "I believe!" He wanted prayer. His name was Yuen Hing.

A drug pusher approached me next. He told me that he wanted to believe in Christ but lacked confidence. He was a big man. He showed me scars on his arms and belly from knife fights. He said, "When I want money, I threaten people. They give it to me." I told him that Christ would accept him if he repented. He said that he was incapable. He became like a child, bunching himself together, shuffling his feet, smiling uncomfortably, and wringing his hands together. I told him how I ran from God and pleaded inability to believe in God when I was a teenager, but that Romans 1:20 says there is no excuse for unbelief. Unbelief is rebellion. God wants all men to be saved. "All you have to do is RECEIVE the grace of God. [20] GOD will give you a new heart; a new life; a new confidence and a new power to overcome your old habits." He was ready! He went with Christians from Hang Fook Camp for treatment and to learn about JESUS.

---

[20] Ephesians 2:8-10

As I was leaving the park, I spotted a man who had mocked me the night before while I preached. He prayed to receive Christ. Two brothers had their arms around his shoulders. They prayed with him.

July 25 was a night of answered prayers. When Christians unite in the name of the Father, Son and Holy Spirit, miracles happen. Incidentally, the Christians who did this outreach prayed for two hours before they started witnessing. Many people believed in Christ. There were similar outreaches planned for this park on August 1, 8· and 15. Local Christians planned to start a church near Temple Street. [Yes indeed, later a church was planted near the park. Local people started calling Temple Street Jesus Street.]

Kay Arthur from Precept Ministries led an inductive Bible study seminar between August 20 – 22. 130 people attended the seminar. The Arthur's and the Bird's went into the PRC with our family. We met a Christian woman named Patty who gave us her address. We handed out Gospel tracts to the people.

A 29-member Big Band from Australia did evangelism with me in the PRC, at Temple Street Park and in a public housing area in HK. We met a man named Mr. Tsui. He suffered from leg trouble for two-years. His wife assembled can openers for $3 per day. Other family members arranged plastic flowers and clipped stray threads from clothing to make money. These poor people lived in a room with 80 square feet of floor space. Their walls and roofs were made of tin. Their community shared one bath and one toilet. They waited 5-7 years to be moved into a larger apartment by the government.

A pastor of an Alliance Church said of our evangelism seminar, "Not one minute was wasted. Everything was applicable and useful. Now, I think we must take time to absorb all that we learned. People have professed Christ already." A professor from the Lutheran Seminary brought one student and one guest to join our Temple Street evangelistic outreach.

Tessie Tchino studied the Bible with Sherry and me in a park after church. It was very hot and humid outside. Tessie was a new Christian. She was a maid. She had 12 free hours per week. She was not allowed to use the telephone where she lived. She was not allowed to have a key to the house. She was concerned for her sister Aveline who was a medium. Her family members were into spiritism.

Our entire family had flu and fever this month. Glory had pneumonia. Sherry cared for two sick babies while being sick herself. Despite her difficult week, she still did Bible study with Happy and Miew Tsang on Saturday. On Saturday afternoon, Sherry taught 10 students English at the Ma Tau Wai Church. Though she felt bad. The Lord blessed her to lead William Lau (age 18) to renew his relationship with Christ. On July 30, Lemuel and I visited William. He was quite excited to talk about Jesus and to pray with us. Our meeting with him lasted more than two hours. We laid hands on William and prayed that the Holy Spirit would fill him. He thanked God several times and exclaimed, "This was the most exciting meeting I ever attended."

Anne Hepburn moved out from our apartment. She has an apartment and bookstore near Temple Street Park. God answered your prayers for her. She was grateful. Christians used her store to counsel the Temple Street Park converts.

Siu Ming (Ah Ming) joined me and others to preach in a public area. He handed out Gospel tracts with enthusiasm. We were joined by Africans from Ethiopia, Liberia, Botswana, Uganda, and Nigeria. They sang and did dramas while Ah Ming and I distributed tracts. As I preached, a policeman appeared. He told me to end my message in two sentences. I obeyed. More than 100 people had gathered to listen. The police officer could not explain to us why we were breaking the law. The Urban Council was curtailing Christians from witnessing in public places. Ah Ming continued to boldly distribute Gospel literature. Though he was skinny and only five-feet tall, God made him a mighty man of valor for Christ.

As we considered moving into the PRC, we made some calculations. My Cantonese was fluent enough to accomplish daily tasks. Sherry had learned how to cook with local vegetables. Anne Hepburn was willing to check our HK mailbox and hold our mail for us. People from RCC in HK were willing to bring us provisions that we could not purchase inside the PRC.

After I resigned my position at YFC to move into the PRC, Zhongshan University informed me that I might have to wait three more months before starting my job. I considered submitting applications at other universities. Mr. Chen Yong and Mr. Lin were the directors of Foreign Affairs at Zhongshan University. The English Department had approved my application for hire, but the Foreign Affairs directors had to approve it. When we visited the Foreign Affairs office, we learned that Director Chen Yong Pei had been on vacation until two days before we arrived. He said that he would process my visa and sponsorship letter within the next two weeks.

During our trip, we met a mother with a baby in arms. She was barefooted. I shared Christ with her. She did not know who Jesus Christ was. She could not understand the Gospel. I tried to give her a tract, but she could not read.

The people in the PRC were generally excited when we shared Christ with them. They had difficult lives. For example, women washing clothes in buckets under the hot sun. Men breaking rocks with chisels and hammers. A 13-year-old boy shoveling concrete in the heat of day. Despite the tropical heat, most had neither air conditioning nor fan. They appreciated us sharing with them about a God who loved them.

On August 18, seven Bible couriers were separately stopped and questioned at length by Public Security Bureau (PSB) agents for religious activities. They were accused of contravening Article 36 of the PRC's constitution. Article 36 states: "No national organ or social organization or person is allowed to force the citizens to believe or not to believe in a religion, and not to discriminate against citizens who believe or not believe in any religion. The nation will protect normal religious activities. But no one is allowed to use religion to disrupt social order, or damage the health of the people, or to interfere with the national education system. Religious organizations are not allowed to be controlled by foreign powers."

The couriers mentioned above were stopped after they passed through customs and on their way to the train station. They were not proselytizing, not preaching, but were detained. Some were questioned for seven hours. Others for 48-hours! Their responses were video recorded. They were charged with bringing Bibles into the PRC which the officials said was illegal.

A 20-year-old HK national named Alex entered the PRC through the Lo Wu border. He was detained at the border for having a Christian songbook and a Christian testimonial book. No Bibles! The guards confiscated these books and released Alex after 13-minutes. He boarded a train for Guangzhou. Shortly, after he arrived in Guangzhou, two men in plain clothes grabbed him and escorted him to a waiting car on a side street. They identified themselves to him as PSB agents and took him to their office. They questioned and threatened Alex for nine hours. They wanted to know the address and phone number of his church in HK. They wanted to know who his pastor was and how many full-time workers were in his church. They wanted to know why he brought Bibles into the PRC. He was warned not to tell anyone of his detention. They kept him in Guangzhou for four days. They took

$283 from him. They made him sign a note that he had willingly gave them the money. He had not. They told him to cooperate, or they would detain him for seven years until the PRC assumed sovereignty over HK.

Though intimidated by the communists, the Christians did not cease preaching the Gospel. They turned to the Lord as the apostles did in Acts 4:24-33. They believed the words of Psalm 2.

Three donors amazed us with great generosity during September. They gave $750 between them which compares with a total of $500 from all other supporters during the previous month. In response to their generosity, we shared offerings with Gospel preachers in Nepal, Malaysia, Poland, Philippines, and the PRC.

On September 22, Happy, Pui Man, Kam, Pak Kai, Yeuk Hong, Cindy, Catherine, and Siu Ying prepared and brought dinner to us including a big cake to farewell us from HK. It was nice that they appreciated Sherry's labors love on their behalf.

Cheng Yu Man told us that he got a job. We helped him out with meals, clothes and took him to The Salvation Army for a place to stay. The last we heard from him was September 4. He told us that he would come to church, but never showed up.

RCC asked us to help with a church plant at their Ma Tau Wai reading center. Sherry taught boys ages 6-11 of servanthood. We used Bible study materials from Christ for the Nations. Jorge Froes and another girl helped me to teach the boys. Our Sunday school activities included Bible reading and memorization.

Jackie Pullinger sponsored John Perry to come to HK. John Perry was the lead guitarist for the Cliff Richard's band. The worship seminar was good. We enjoyed worshipping the Lord.

Our one-year-old daughter, Glory, walked by holding onto things. Grace was a real joy to me. She was a beautiful but stubborn character. She loved to play dolls. When she played, she involved everyone around her with her pretending. It was serious stuff! She sang praises to God and encouraged us to sing along. She sang the Chinese song. "Jyu Yehsou jan keihmiu" – "Isn't He wonderful." She could almost sing the entire ABC song but did not recognize all the letters yet. She enjoyed using the tambourine while singing praises.

Smiles and good deeds happened often between the food market hawkers and ourselves. We invited them to evangelistic meetings at YFC, but they did not come. We prayed for them. Once, I heard them yelling as they ran from the social service officers. It was as if they were in hell crying which burdened me.

Sherry spoke with Pu Cho on the phone recently. She moved to Tsim Tsa Tsui. Her baby was due to be born in December. Sherry hoped to see her before we moved to the PRC. She would not respond to Jesus. When Sherry shared with her, she became quiet and changed the subject.

The YFC staff members showed us much kindness before we left HK. The Bible study group returned twice to see us before we moved to the PRC. Siu Ying professed faith in Christ. Others gave us their addresses. They asked us to write them.

Between October 1 – 4, we helped Janny Fong witness to her relatives. The Lord used Janny to lead her cousin (Kwan) to Christ before we arrived. Then, Miss Yu, another cousin believed. While we sat on a bench and prayed for converts, a man came up to us, and listened to the Gospel. Then, two more boys joined us. Finally, all three strangers prayed to receive Christ as their Savior. Sherry and Janny witnessed to another cousin named Yok Lan. At the very moment that Yok Lan prayed to Christ, Grace, Glory, and I saw a large snake swim across the lake. He started from the place where Yok Lan was seated. It was as if the devil had departed from her. We rejoiced!

On the morning that we moved to Guangzhou, I read, "Worthy is the Lamb, who was slain, to receive power and wealth and wisdom and strength and honor and glory and praise."[21] May the Holy Spirit work through us in such a way that many Chinese shall say, "Worthy is the Lamb to receive everything I have."

Jesus gave me 23 students to care for at Zhongshan University. Seven of these 23 talked with me after class. Xian asked to visit me personally. Jia Jie was friendly. Three students complimented me on my teaching methods. Glory to God! I used Precept Ministry methods to teach a reading comprehension course. I witnessed to my students. For example, I explained the meaning of the word "reconcile." Another time, I explained the meaning of the word "theory." "Theory is a belief. If the

---

[21] Revelation 5:12

postulation is supported by the evidence, then it is a fact not a theory." I taught them, "Evolution lacks evidence, so it is a theory or belief." Zhongshan had a statue of Charles Darwin. Their curriculum was pro-evolution and pro-atheism.

Eugene Lee, a cousin of a former YFC staff member lived and studied at this university. He planned to visit us weekly. He thoroughly heard the Gospel this week. He seemed to absorb it.

We prayed that God would protect those who visited us. The heads of the Foreign Affairs Office (Mr. Fung and Mrs. Qin) had already pulled a surprise visit on us once. They said that they wanted to deliver something to us but scoped out our living quarters. Mr. Fung told me that he and his colleagues studied party policy every Thursday.

The Lord provided us a large apartment via my job. Grace was happy. She sang, "Jesus is coming." A song that we never heard before! Our food was $1 per meal at the school cafeteria. It was often floating in oil. We ate it to save money. The water had to be boiled before being drank due to the high level in bacteria it.

During the first quarter, I taught four hours per week and received $150 per month, plus utilities and accommodations. I did not mind the light workload because I used my free time to meet with people. We visited Miss Hong Ying, a Russian named Michael and a Japanese named Zhou Juk. We gave them tracts.

At night, we had to cover our beds with mosquito nets. The mosquitos spread a disease. 28 people were hospitalized due to this disease. Once, Sherry found a large tarantula on the side of

71

a suitcase after she had just reached inside of it. Americans David and Patti gave us flea spray to kill the spider. It worked.

On October 24, we encountered a beggar girl. Her feet and hands were black with dirt. We gave her ice cream. She only held onto it. She kept on begging. She did not eat it. Sherry guessed that her "owners" must beat her to make her afraid to do anything that they had not permitted her to do. The next day, we gave her five thick cookies. We gave her a beautiful coat to replace the filthy rag of coat that she wore. She took the gifts. I gave her a Gospel tract. She examined the picture of Jesus on the cross. A vendor told us that the girl had a mother but no father. On the third day, we brought a children's book in Chinese to give to her but found her older sister begging in her place.

During November, Sherry wrote to her parents, saying, "I have been thinking of you so often lately because I feel like I am you in many situations. I find myself responding as you do. Grace and Glory are growing fast. Glory gave us hope for her development when she walked five steps. Praise the Lord! This brings tremendous joy to me. I prayed, 'Father, Jesus please let Glory walk. You can cause her to do it today even though it doesn't look like she can.' Nothing is too hard for God. Glory is very timid in some ways so up to this point she has been fearful to even stand by herself yet has displayed to us that she has been quite capable of standing and walking. She now says 'dat' meaning "that" and points at what she wants. She shakes her head yes and no at the right times. She also says 'Mama' as if to say

'Hey, I need this.' She also says 'Dada' for Mark. She waves goodbye, folds her hands to pray, gives bear hugs, kisses, smiles and she laughs a lot. She also likes to climb just like Louise did. Glory loves Grace a lot and depends on Grace to help her out with things and of course Grace just loves to be a good big sister. It blesses my heart to watch them play together and laugh or see them hug and kiss each other without being told to do so. It reminds me of how much I loved Jami, Louise and Sara when I was growing up."

"Grace has grown physically and spiritually. She looks more like Mark and uses many of his gestures. She's three feet tall and weighs 26 pounds. She uses chop sticks fluently. She even picks up peanuts and puts them in her mouth. But the greatest growth is in her spirit. She says, 'I'm sorry' genuinely when she knows she's done wrong and feels bad for it. She told me about Jesus on her birthday. First, she asked, 'Mom, tell me the story 'bout Jesus.' I said, 'You tell me.' So, she said, 'Pilate said, 'Are You the Son of God?' Jesus said, 'I am.' 'Soldiers hands and feet (she did the actions of nailing hands and feet). Buried Him! Three days He rose again.' I was surprised she knew the sequence and seemed to understand it."

"One-day last week, Grace said to Glory, 'Glory, Jesus knows Gracey's heart.' I was flabbergasted. These were the words of a mature person and yet she said it so simply."

"Grace usually sings praise songs while riding on buses. She has everyone's attention as she sings, claps, and lifts her hands. Grace also prayed for Jesus to heal me. I had a sore that was infected. I was talking about how it hurt. Grace and I were alone. She said, 'Let me pray for it.' So, I said okay and sat down by her. She put her hand on me and looked at me so that I would start the prayer. I said, 'Dear Jesus' and she repeated and then added, 'Help Mommy.' And then I said, 'In Jesus' Name.' And she said, 'Amen.' The next day it was better."

"Grace also surprised me when one of Mark's students came for an appointment. Mark was temporarily gone. The student wanted to stay at least 30-minutes to see if Mark would come home. Mark did not return for 40-minutes. Grace began to talk with him about Jesus. She got her Bible story book out and began to show him pictures and explain to the pictures to him. She told him, 'Jesus is real.' Then, she turned to the page where Jesus was walking on the water and said exactly that. Next, she pointed to Jesus touching and healing a lame man. She said, 'See Jesus is touching the boy, and now he is better.' I was surprised. This student was a philosophy professor at the university. He was searching for the truth. He listened to Grace the whole time."

"As for Mark, I could not ask for no better. I am very thankful that the Lord yoked him to me. He is a continual blessing. He is a very good husband to me and a very good dad to Grace and Glory. He seems to be overwhelmed often with concerns but overcomes through Christ who gives him strength."

"The Lord has given Mark a brother in the faith to encourage him. This brother's name is Robert Weathersby. He is probably 40 years old. He is from Mississippi. They pray together daily for at least an hour. I am thankful for Robert because I am often too busy to encourage Mark with Bible verses. Robert reads the Bible a lot. When they get together, they talk about the Bible and are aglow afterwards. There are other Christian teachers with families in Mark's department. They are like family to us."

I added a postscript note to Sherry's letter, saying, "After Grace heard the Gospel and of the outpouring of the Holy Spirit, she wanted to ask Jesus in her heart. She prayed a prayer after me. She asked God to forgive her sins and Jesus to make His home in her heart. One week later, late at night, while carrying her to get a drink of water, she asked me, 'Why is Jesus in Grace's heart?' Her life shows the fruit of a born-again believer. She carries the Bible around. Sometimes she sits in her plastic chair and looks at the pages of my Bible. She does this for long periods of time. Praise God! This is God's doing."

I also wrote a letter to Sherry's parents about our family, saying, "Grace always talks about going to see her cousins Josiah, Christopher and Jacob. She listened to the cassette tape that Louise sent daily for hours. We play with Grace a lot to offset her loneliness. We bought Grace a beautiful bicycle with training wheels for $15. We are now looking to buy her a dollhouse with money that you and others sent for her birthday. We bought both daughters dolls. Glory likes Grace's bicycle and dolls. She likes to walk while holding onto furniture. We take hour-long bus rides to a park where they can play. We hand out Gospel tracts together.

Grace usually gets an ice cream to eat on the way home. She talks about the little beggar girl at the park on our way home."

"Sherry encourages me when I get anxious about saying the wrong thing at the wrong moment. The other Christian teachers called a meeting with us after an unbelieving American girl accused me of forcing religion on people. Sherry urged me to speak all that the Lord tells me to say. We thoroughly shared the Gospel with a student named Eugene Lee when he visited us."

On November 23, I was asked to share impromptu at a Christian meeting with nearly 70 Chinese in attendance. The Holy Spirit led me to share from Matthew 6:25, 33 and Revelation 21. While I taught, men in black suits came and stood in the doorway and took pictures. At this same meeting on an earlier occasion, one of these men tied in with these men had taken pictures of Grace and Glory, as well as wrote down our address. At the close of the meeting, Grace tugged at Sherry's leg, saying, "Mommy, I have to go pee-pee." Sherry handed Glory to me. Just in that instant, Grace was gone. We immediately started searching and calling out for Grace. Sherry spotted two of the men in black walking Grace down the stairwell toward the exit. She yelled, "No way! No way! Grace, don't go with them… they are bad!" They kept walking. Sherry flew down the stairs and pulled Grace from their hands. One of the men followed Sherry back up the stairs. Sherry told me while the man was still looking at Grace, "He tried to take Grace out the door." The man denied it. "Yes, you did." Sherry replied. He only laughed. She told him, "Jesus is Lord!" I

76

was silent. Who could I call on for justice except for God? We told Sister Kathy what happened. We asked her to have Christians in HK pray for us. We left the meeting place with no further hinderance. Praise the Lord! He watched over Grace.

Days before this incident happened, I told Sherry, "I feel it is a matter of life or death that we have devotions with Grace and Glory every morning and evening, and that we pray for the Lord to protect them." Another Christian had prayed for them as well.

On the night of the meeting, I had a strong feeling that the meeting would be disrupted. We needed to stop our busy tasks before going and pray earnestly for our protection and our ability to proclaim Jesus' Name no matter what happened. Sherry did speak the Name of Jesus to the men who tried to take Grace.

Our initial reaction to this incident was to want to flee the country as Mary and Joseph fled from Herod, but we waited. We asked the Lord lead our response. The Lord spoke to Sherry via Exodus 14:13-14. This was during the early hours of the next morning. The crux of this passage was that the enemies we had seen, we would see no more. We had peace to stay.

After this incident, the foreign affairs office called me in for questioning. As far as I knew, they were not informed about what happened. They asked me questions about my background and about the places I had visited in the PRC. I told them very little, but they seemed content. To our surprise, these officers were nice to us after this questioning. They no longer frowned at us. They started greeting us. God answered our prayers.

Glory started walking on Sunday, November 22, the day before the incident at the Saan Yu Bing Guan. Three local Christians joined us for worship. I shared with them from Revelation 5:7-13 about how Jesus is worthy of our lives. These Christians continued to meet with us.

I gave a pamphlet by Josh McDowell to my students. It contained evidence for the empty tomb of Jesus Christ. After that, 12 students talked with me for 90-minutes about Christianity. The Gospel was shared. Most of these students were scientists who hoped to study in the US. After talking with these students, I praised God for His amazing grace.

James Zhong visited me three times because he wanted to know more about God. Thanks to some HK Christians, I was able to gift James with a cassette tape that had a teaching in Chinese on it by Derek Prince. The title of the message was "What is Truth?" James was married to woman's whose father was a communist party member. We prayed that his hunger for truth would be greater than his fear of the communist party.

Anne Hepburn's Dayspring Bookstore was a refuge for us when we visited HK. She let us leave our suitcases at her shop while we did our banking and postal business. Our trips to HK involved an overnight boat ride on Friday evenings and a train ride on Saturday afternoons back to the PRC. Anne held our incoming mail for us. Anne made us feel welcome. We appreciated her. The tracts and Josh McDowell books that we distributed came from her store. We also gave street children illustrated Bible story books from her store.

Zhongshan University gave me more teaching hours. I taught 13 hours per week. I had 45 students. The quarter ended on January 31, 1988.

In a letter to friends, I wrote, "Some of the Scriptures that the Lord gave me this month were Daniel 7:14 and Isaiah 9:6-7. These passages speak of the sovereignty of Christ over rulers and kingdoms. The Lord gave Sherry Proverbs 27:10, and Psalm 116:6. God encouraged us greatly via Bible meditation. Robert Weathersby also prayed with us and encouraged us daily."

During December, Louise discipled Nancy almost daily. Nancy was a laboratory technician in her 40's. She used her vacation time to learn more about Jesus. Nancy was baptized in our bathtub and joined the home fellowship.

Sherry, Louise, Grace, and Glory made a trip to HK. They returned with 10 inductive Bible study books by Precept Ministries, as well as more children's illustrated Bible story books in Chinese. We gave the people four hours of training on "How to Study Your Bible" with these books. We gave James Zhong the entire book of "Evidence that Demands a Verdict" in Chinese, plus a cassette tape of Christian music by Mike Adkins. The album was entitled, "Thank you for the Dove." He told us that Christian music made him happy. James did a return favor for us. He led us to an orphanage where we distributed Christian tapes and Bible story books to the children. Praise the Lord!

~ Chapter 5 ~
Called by the Gospel (1988)

The Holy Spirit led us to pray for the people that we encountered. Five believed in Christ during January, one was baptized and five attended our "house church" twice weekly. Dr. Shao Befun was baptized in our bathtub by Robert. She was a medical doctor. Robert shared the Gospel with her.

I returned to the Saan Yu Bing Guan for another meeting. Two of the Christians told me that they enjoyed the Bible study methods that I taught from Revelation 21. "Can you teach us the Bible?" they asked. Chung Kwa and Soon Ying started joining our Bible meetings.

The Lord used Warren and Louise to lead Shao Ying to Christ. They discipled her and two others in our apartment. These training sessions usually lasted more than two hours due to the eagerness of the ladies to study God's Word.

Cathy Lam shared with us that her father was imprisoned for five years during the Cultural Revolution due to political reasons. Her mother was committed to a mental hospital. Her 10-year-old brother, Yat Keung, wandered the streets alone. She and her sister were raised for 10 years by a couple appointed by the government. Cathy's parents allowed us to meet in their home despite their past sufferings. Her father was kindhearted. Before I finished drinking my cup of tea, he poured me another cup. He constantly offered his guests orange slices. Yat Keung believed in Christ on December 20, last year.

The Christian meeting where I shared from Revelation 21 and where Grace was nearly kidnapped was cancelled by the authorities in February. The American pastors were detained for questioning. Other missionaries were released after their identities were recorded. The officer warned the Christians not to listen to foreign missionaries. They reminded them to only attend government sanctioned churches. They ordered them to leave. One of the arresting officers said that an outsider lodged a complaint against this illegal meeting.

Sherry and I had planned to attend the "illegal" meeting, but the Holy Spirit stopped us. We waited at a bus stop in front of our university. We waited a long time. No bus came. Our spirits felt unsettled. When we prayed about the lack of peace in our hearts, we determined that it was the Holy Spirit urging us not to join the meeting. We praised God for stopping us. If we had been arrested, the government probably would have cancelled my teaching position at the university and blacklisted us from returning to the PRC for a couple of years. We praised God that no local Christians were imprisoned. They were released without having to show the authorities their identification.

Two American pastors baptized 18 new believers on Friday, January 9. Three of these believers began attending our Bible meeting. What did the believers from our fellowship do after the police raided that meeting at the Saan Yu Bing Guan?

They showed up at our next meeting ready to learn more about Jesus. They were more excited about Jesus after their persecution experience than they were beforehand. The Lord led me to share with them from Psalm 23 that night. Jesus is the Good Shepherd. He blesses those who experience persecution. He promised us a place in His house and at His table forever.

During the last classes of my second quarter, Sherry sang the song, "Because He lives." She explained the meaning of the song to one class of 24 students and to another class of 50. Sherry made a spaghetti dinner for the Christians who attended our in-home Bible meeting.

On Friday, I preached at the Temple Street Park in HK. Lee Chi Wa gave his life to Jesus and received the life of Jesus in return. And what's more, I saw Wai Leung there. He was giving out tracts. He committed his life to Jesus last year when I preached at RCC. The Lord's grace and love is amazing.

"I will sing to the Lord all my life; I will sing praise to my God as long as I live. May my meditation be pleasing to Him, as I rejoice in the Lord." [22] On April 19, Sherry shared this verse as well as Psalm 103:1-2, 4-5, 10, 12; Psalm 105:4-5; and Psalm 34:1-2 at a meeting of the Lutheran Women's Missionary League. It was less than 12-hours before our departure from St. Louis to HK. Praising and blessing the Lord is a choice that God has given us the power to make. Just like we can say, "I will eat" or "I will

---

[22] Psalm 104:33-34 NIV

not eat." In Christ we can say, "I will bless the Lord at all times: His praise shall continually be in my mouth." [23] Sherry shared that singing praises to God and being glad in Him is her strength. She ended her sharing with the verse, "O taste and see that the Lord is good: blessed is the man that trusts in Him." [24] The ladies responded with gratitude for her sharing. Praise God!

On April 10, I was officially ordained for the Gospel ministry that I'm doing in the PRC by the pastor and elders of Living Faith Center in Ashland, Missouri. The Holy Spirit led them to do this for me. I thanked God for this high calling.

Kari Mitchell and Nancy Davidson committed their lives to Jesus while we were in the US. Nancy was baptized at Troy Christian Church. Praise the Lord!

The Lord got us back to HK after a brief trip to the US. I returned to my teaching post at Zhongshan University on May 6. We were grateful to Sherry's parents, my parents, Sherry's sisters Jami and Louise, as well as for Marvin and Beverly Moore, Twain and Donna Hill, and for Wally and Irene Kutz. They provided accommodations for us. We had no home, car, or property in the US. Their hospitality was a tremendous blessing to us. Sherry's parents and sister Louise also let us use their cars to make three trips to Columbia, Missouri, one trip to Chicago, Illinois, and one trip to LaPorte, Indiana.

---

[23] Psalm 34:1 NIV
[24] Psalm 34:8 NIV

Louise did not return with us to the PRC. She started work with The Salvation Army in Belleville, Illinois. She continued to evangelize and disciple people.

John Su, the first believer to join our Bible meeting in the PRC, successfully immigrated to the US on April 25. His spouse and relatives were already there. We got to visit with John twice before he departed. It was 5 pm on Sunday when he came to us. He had not eaten that day. He only had one dollar. The Lord moved us to give him $50 traveling money. John beamed with faith in Christ. He wrote us later to say, "It is a miracle that God brought you into our home to preach the Gospel. Now, we have entered a new world. Happiness and strength have come to our hearts. Praise God!"

12 of my university students wrote me while we were in the US. Zheming wrote, "There are countless twists and turns in life. Everyone needs a spiritual pillar. God and Jesus are a spiritual pillar. I know very little about Jesus, but I want to learn more." Deng Hong wrote, "While at home, I found a book about the Bible in Chinese. I am now reading it and finding it interesting. It is easier to read than the Bible printed in English."

On Sunday, April 24, we met William Lau (age 19) and Siu Ming (age 16) at RCC. These were converts that the Lord used us to lead to Him. They faithfully attended church services. RCC's services lasted two and half hours. They were hungry for Jesus. Siu Ming asked us to pray for his mother and brother. His mother suffered from mental illness. His brother was physically abusive towards him.

Mirasol & Vicente Hernando wrote to us from the Philippines. Mirasol took our evangelism and follow-up seminar while in HK. She wrote, "The first day of the evangelism seminar was marvelous due to the enabling power of the Holy Spirit. Pastors Vicente (my husband), Billy and Rufino are helping me teach the seminar. We taught the people in the Ilocano dialect. The people thirst for training. Thank God for making you instrumental in preparing this Evangelism Training Manual, and for training me so I could in turn train others for the Gospel and for the lost." Jami, Sherry's sister, asked us to channel a $75 donation from her to these pastors. So, we split the $75 between pastors Vincente ($15), Billy ($20), Rufino ($20) and Cesar Mangsat in Saipan ($20). Praise God! The Gospel went forth!

As I mentioned earlier, Sherry spoke at a Lutheran Church in Chicago to a women's missionary league. She spoke about praising the Lord! Afterwards, she felt a bit nauseous. That was her first indication that she was pregnant. She was due to give birth in November. She conceived at a time when praising God was all she wanted to do! We were overjoyed! Thank You Lord!

In May, Jesus gave me the opportunity to pray for a former student's healing. Doctors could not relieve Guo Rong's neck pain. I prayed for his neck in the name of Jesus. Later that evening, he said his neck was better. Zhe Ming came with him.

Sherry taught English to Nancy and Miss Chow. Nancy was a believer, but Miss Chow heard the Gospel for the first time from Sherry. Nancy's co-workers opposed her for learning English. She told Sherry, "I just want to die." We made a special trip to see her. We urged friends to pray for these two ladies.

A civil engineer and former student of mine named Deng Hong telephoned me. He said that he wanted to know more about Jesus. So, I invited him over. Six days later, I had the privilege to lead him to Jesus at a Gospel meeting. He gave his life to Jesus even though people connected to the government were forbidden to do so. He returned to us two days after his conversion with two-hours-worth of questions to ask us about Jesus. He and his girlfriend attended discipleship classes and worship services. His girlfriend had not yet believed in Jesus.

Mandy was one of four women that Sherry gave Bible lessons to on Sundays. She wanted to be a missionary to Saipan. She believed that there were many Chinese in Saipan.

James asked me to be the godfather of his two-year-old son (Tse Zhang). He wanted his son to be a Christian and for me to disciple him. Ironically, he and his wife were not yet converted.

More Bible story books were given to the children at the Zhiling school. Wai Na, the principal of Zhiling, urged me to visit a famous radio announcer named Thomas Wan. He recently suffered a nervous breakdown and needed healing.

Lindsay is a nine-year-old American girl. She is the daughter of one of the American teachers at Zhongshan

University. Lindsay believed in Indian gods, myths, and Jesus, but her interest in Jesus increased. Once while Lindsay and Grace played together, Grace said to Sherry, "Mom, I'm showing her what to read and she's reading it (Bible stories). I'm telling Lindsay what God told me to say." They read Bible stories with one another on three occasions.

The Chinese people we knew lived on $40 per month. Our family ate basic foods such as vegetables, fruit, bean curd, fish, and oatmeal, and still spent $60 per month. Our $60 did not include the relatively expensive box of juices that we purchased for Grace and Glory. We learned that Gong Ming worked three jobs to support himself and pay his college fees. In contrast to food expenses, housing and utilities was subsidized by the government. Transportation was nearly free (bicycles).

We found William Lau doing tract ministry at Temple Street Park with the RCC outreach team. The Lord had previously used Sherry to lead him to Christ. Glory to God!

Zhongshan University told me that they were cutting five teaching positions including mine and would not invite me back to teach in the fall. I was sad. I cried out desperately to Jesus for a miracle. I wanted to remain in the PRC.

Before I finished teaching my classes, I received a visit from three officials of the South China Agricultural University. They came to my apartment and offered me a position and a $40 raise over what Zhongshan had offered me. I had applied there. Sherry liked the housing there. I had not heard from them in so long that I assumed that they would not hire me. Incidentally, I had prayed that I could help China's farmers. This new position would open that door for me.

In Shenzhen, I saw an elderly woman carrying three bags on a bamboo pole that was resting on her shoulder. The pole was bowing under the weight and so was her back. I started to help her, but then, realized that carrying luggage was her method of earning income. In the fields along the railway, farmers worked without machinery. They carried large buckets of water on both ends of a bamboo pole supported by their shoulders. The climate was tropical. How could I help undo their heavy burdens? I would help my university students on their path towards mechanizing these jobs that required heavy lifting. I encouraged those on their way to study in the US to return to help the poor.

The Lord cares for the poor. He asked us. "Is not this the kind of fasting I have chosen: to loosen the chains of injustice and untie the cords of the yoke, to set the oppressed free and break every yoke? Is it not to share your food with the hungry and to provide the poor wanderer with shelter—when you see the naked, to clothe them, and not to turn away from your own flesh and blood?" [25]

Recently, a large crowd gathered around us as we were walking a sidewalk. They were interested in Grace and Glory. Our little daughters looked like dolls to them. The Holy Spirit

---

[25] Isaiah 58:6-7 NIV

compelled me to hand booklets to them by Josh McDowell entitled, "Evidence for the Resurrection of Jesus Christ." The crowd rushed to grab the booklets from me. A whole stack was gone in 60 seconds. Sherry gave out 10 children's illustrated Bible books in less than a minute. A minute of time had the potential to change a life forever.

On May 16, a visiting ministry team prayed for the local believers. Some began to speak in tongues including my fellow teacher, Robert Weathersby. Robert's excitement was so great that he stayed up very late praising Jesus. Rose had a vision of a glassy sea. She heard heavenly voices singing praises to Jesus.

The Lord reconnected us with James. He had not believed but had developed a friendship with a respected Christian writer and teacher. God had him surrounded. James did us a favor. He led us to the Zhiling school for special needs children.

We inherited disciples from the Saan Yu Bing Guan meeting that was disbanded by the police. They were hungry for Jesus and His Word. We prayed for their spiritual growth.

Yesterday, Sherry tripped on steps while carrying boiling hot drinking water from downstairs. She prayed as she was falling, and even though she fell and the water soaked her legs, she was unhurt. Today, She had a doctor checkup. Baby (Andrew) was fine. She was three months pregnant.

During the month of July, I read James 1:27. The Holy Spirit brought me to my knees afterwards. I asked God to forgive me for neglecting widows and orphans. 10 days later, God led us to a Christian widow's home. Her English name was Lydia. With tears streaming down her face, Lydia told me her story:

> In January this year, my husband got cancer. The hospital couldn't help him. I called a Christian friend who said she would pray. Then, a Christian doctor arrived. My third daughter believed in Jesus after he told her the Gospel. Then, my husband and me believed. My husband died in April (she could barely speak between sobs and all three daughters were crying). After my husband died, he had a beautiful smile on his face. I know this was Jesus.
>
> My husband had saved and borrowed a total sum of $1,700 to start a restaurant, but his colleague took the money. I had to take the man to court. The entire amount was given to us. This was Jesus.
>
> My birthday was June 10. I was dreading this day. I didn't know how to face it. Then, a missionary who spoke at our house church came to visit us on June 10. I was so happy. Today, July 3, would've been my husband's birthday. I was also dreading this day, but now, God has brought you and your family to us. I know this is Jesus. I am so happy today.

We talked about Jesus and studied the Bible together for five hours. As I typed Lydia's testimony, I realized her birthday was on the 15th anniversary of my father's death. I had said to the Lord during my father's funeral that I wanted HIM (the Lord) to use my life to comfort the bereaved with the Gospel. I felt at that time that God would either call me to China or to Africa or both. Here I was in China, comforting a bereaved widow. Our Lord answered the silent prayer that I prayed at age 13.

During August, Lydia and her three daughters, Linda, Persis, and Mercy did Bible studies with us on a weekly basis. They had two visitors from Xinjiang Province. One of them told us, "As you prayed, Jesus spoke to me and said, "Surely, I am in this place." When he said this, it was as though Jesus said it Himself. Just days before this meeting, I had prayed that God would raise up prophets in the PRC who could hear His voice and speak His Word. I gave Mr. Sung from Xinjiang a booklet on the major doctrines of the Bible.

Last month, believers pedaled their bikes for 60-minutes in 90-degree weather with 95% humidity to join our Bible study. Three weeks ago, we had five attendees, last Sunday we had 10. One doctor was healed of shoulder pain after being prayed for. The disciples took notes during the Bible study. They asked questions about what they learned at the end of the study time.

I finished my first year of teaching at Zhongshan. After that, I picked up a temporary teaching position at a YMCA evening school in HK. Peter and Jean Cameron from Australia invited us to stay in their spare bedroom for the summer. My teaching position at the South China Agricultural University was to begin on August 26.

While we stayed with Peter and Jean Cameron, they took in a 15-year-old girl who was demonized. They rebuked the demons from her in the Name of Jesus. Afterwards, she professed Jesus. Before she was set free, she had gone 14-days without sleeping and 10-days without eating. She was emaciated when she arrived. She would groan, yell, hiss, cough and stare wide-eyed at us. At first, Sherry was concerned for the safety of our children, but God led us to stay and pray for the girl whose name was Yuen Pui. Five days and nights went by. Peter and Jean had little sleep. At times, they lost their appetites and fasted. They prayed fervent prayers for her. At times, Yuen Pui's body would be stiff, and her face would be contorted. Sometimes it would take more than an hour of prayer to calm her down when the demons were at work. A missionary prayer chain was initiated. Finally, on the sixth day of being in the Cameron's apartment, the last demon left her.

Yuen Pui ate and slept again. She praised the Lord. She smiled, sang, and held tightly to her Bible. She asked her father to forgive her for the bad things she had done. The Lord set a captive free through the spiritual labors of love by His servants.

During August, a 35-year-old American pastor named Steve Robinson began to accompany me to the PRC. He played a portable piano and led the singing. He shared messages with the group. During one trip, Steve asked me if I could help him apply to teach at a university in the PRC. I replied, "That will take quite a miracle because the school year is about to begin." Then, I added, "But nothing is impossible with God." Steve was a blessing to us. We wanted him to succeed. On the morning that we set out to find Steve a teaching position, I had read Joshua 12:7-24. These verses list the kings that Joshua and his army conquered on the day that the sun stood still. They conquered 31 kings in one day because they depended on the Lord. [26] I told Steve, "I believe the Lord is going to do a miracle today!"

We did much walking that day. It was very hot and humid. Our clothes were soaked with perspiration. My ability to communicate in Cantonese was vital to us. I was ready to give up, but then, the Lord reminded me, "36 kings!" I told Steve, "This is our 36 kings in one-day experience." Within 10 minutes of that confession, we found the home of the English Department Supervisor at the Normal University. We knocked on his door. He invited us in. He was watching, "The Sound of Music." Steve told him that he wanted to apply for a teaching position with the English Department. The man hired Steve on the spot. He said, "We need a teacher desperately. Can you start next week?" Steve took the job. Praise the Lord!

Two years ago, Sherry's sister met Happy. Happy was 17 then. Louise studied the Bible with Happy and her friends. After Louise left, Sherry continued to study with her until we moved to Guangzhou. Before we left HK, Happy started attending English classes at RCC. Sherry briefly taught that class before we left. Happy met April Chan at this class and due to April's friendliness towards her she continued to take the class. On September 11, Happy stood in the baptismal waters at RCC and confessed, "Now, I truly believe in the Lord Jesus. It was not until one month ago that I believed in Him. Through many friends at this church, I

---

[26] See Joshua Chapters 10-11

have learned about His faithfulness to help me and change me."
William Lau, whom Sherry witnessed to at Ma Tau Wai Church
one year ago, was also baptized on September 11. Praise the
Lord!

Robert Weathersby witnessed to our friend James Zhang.
James finally believed in Christ. Robert told us, "James has begun
praying to Jesus." Glory to God!

The Lord blessed us to present 12 study books to Lydia
and her daughters. They completed the studies and took the tests
in the back of the books. We took their test papers to HK where
an Assemblies of God Church worker scored their tests. They did
excellent. The church awarded them with certificates. This made
them happy which made us happy.

In September, we rented a large room at a hotel to hold
our Bible meetings. However, at the end of our second meeting, a
group of men told us that our rental agreement was cancelled.
They were most likely PSB because they spoke with authority.

During October, Mr. Ye and Miss Jade professed faith in
Christ. They prayed to Him for the first time in their lives. We
baptized four from our discipleship group in a lake. Glory to God!

On October 2, I showed the believers on a map where
Nepal was located. I asked them to pray for the Nepalese. Then,
on October 9, one week later, Ginny Anderson from Nepal
showed up suddenly. He got our address from a HK missionary.
We were all amazed at how fast God answered our prayers.

We purchased eight evangelism books from YFC. We gave them to the leaders of our Bible group. We used the books to teach them how to share the Gospel with others.

Recently, one of the believers became pregnant with her second child. She was forced by the government to abort her baby. She was depressed afterwards. Besides this sad news, we learned that girls and handicapped babies were being abandoned. The parents preferred healthy boy babies since they could only have one child per family. There was an orphanage in Guangzhou that had many abandoned children. We hoped to help them soon.

Sherry was almost due to give birth to Andrew. The Lord graciously provided her, her mother, and our daughters rooms in an apartment 10-minutes from the hospital. There was a free bus that went to the supermarket every 30-minutes. Missionaries John and Francene Allen stayed at the same apartment. They felt safe.

Grace and Glory enjoyed being with their grandmother. Grandma adjusted well to unfamiliar food and to inconveniences. Sherry was grateful for her help.

I exited the PRC between 4 pm on Fridays until 6 am on Sundays. This was to enjoy time with my family in HK. I met with believers in Guangzhou on Sunday afternoons.

James Zhang asked me to do a two-hour lecture for his philosophy students at Zhongshan University. My topic was "Religion in America." I was blessed to have 70 students and one police officer attend. One of the students joined our Bible meeting and professed faith in Christ. James asked me to get Church history and doctrine textbooks so that he could include these subjects in his curriculum.

YFC notified me that the Reachout Singers would be staying at the Ocean Hotel in Guangzhou on November 7. By faith, I told my South China Agricultural University (SCAU) students that the singers would perform for them on November 8. My supervisor, Mr. Liu, had granted me permission to have them sing. I rode my bike four miles to the Ocean Hotel only to find out that the singers were not there. Since the Ocean Hotel had International Direct Dialing, I took the opportunity to call Sherry (she was in HK) to see if she had given birth to our son. She was still waiting, BUT she had talked with YFC that day and found out that the Reachout Singers were staying at the White Swan Hotel. So, two 30-minute bus rides and one 15-minute walk later, I arrived at the White Swan Hotel.

I told the Reachout Singers about the opportunity to sing at SCAU. They immediately cancelled all other plans. They eagerly accepted the invitation to sing for my students.

On November 8, the Reachout Singers sang and testified for Jesus at SCAU. About 30 students attended. They also brought Bibles and worship music cassette tapes for the students.

We suffered persecution for our bold witness for Christ. The following Communist Party Members visited me: Mr. Liu, Mr. Cha Zhen Xiong, Mr. Sen, and Ms. Huang. Mr. Liu told me that I broke the PRC's law. He said, "You have been warned!" Ms. Huang commanded me not to hold Bible meetings again. Mr.

Liu began to monitor my classes to ensure that I was not using class time to talk about Jesus.

On Friday, November 18, at 10:33 pm, Andrew was born to us. He weighed seven pounds and fifteen ounces. I was blessed to be standing next to Sherry as he was born. I was praying over her and showering her forehead with kisses. Her labor lasted three hours. We praised God for a son to go with our two daughters.

These was another Reachout Singer concert planned for November 21 at Zhongshan University. 36 of my students from SCAU signed up to attend. These students asked me to teach them more about the Bible.

25 of my SCAU students attended the Zhongshan University concert with the Reachout Singers. They attended even though Mr. Liu had threatened them with severe consequences. He made the students sign a document if they were in favor of Jesus. He said, "Anyone who signs this document will be sent back to their work unit and fail this program." The students came anyway. An American pastor who was arrested previously for preaching the Gospel in the PRC, was our speaker. Some of my students professed faith in Christ. One said that he heard the voice of Jesus speak as the preacher preached. Another said that he felt like crying when he heard how God's Son suffered for our sins.

One of the students who attended the November 21 concert, Mr. O Yang, invited me to his room to hold a Bible study with him. Two nights later, I showed up to study the Bible with him and found seven students besides him waiting for me. Mr. O apologized, saying, "They also wanted to learn the Bible." We studied the Bible and had open dialogue about Christ from 7:30 – 11:00 pm. The students enjoyed the Bibles and worship tapes that the Reachout Singers gave them.

On November 23, I went to the American Consulate in Guangzhou to ask for a copy of the PRC's laws about Christianity. The consul invited me into his office to speak confidentially with me. He said that I was subject to the whims of the local authorities. By hand language and whispering, he indicated to me that his office was bugged with electronic listening devices. He took down a report of what I told him about the persecution of Christians at SCAU. He assured that he would convey my report to the proper authorities. He wrote down his questions and passed them to me. I wrote down my answers and passed them to him. He told me that other teachers in Guangzhou had reported persecution as well.

After I left the Consulate, I went to Zhongshan University to warn Robert Weathersby about what was happening at SCAU. We prayed together. Robert had helped me to plan the Reachout Singers concert. We rejoiced that God had answered our prayers. More than 100 students attended the concert. It was held in an auditorium that I had rented at the Ramada Inn.

Two more people from our Bible study group professed faith in Christ this month. One student whom I taught evangelism methods led a third person to Christ. One new believer shared with me his nightly routine. He said, "First, I listen to Christian radio from HK, then, I read a chapters of the Bible, and finally, I pray over the prayer request cards that you gave me."

I purchased a box of prayer cards from Anne Hepburn's bookstore. I distributed the cards to the believers in Guangzhou. The cards had prayer requests on them for various people groups around the world. They were printed in Chinese. The prayers of these students blessed my heart. They absolutely believed that Jesus heard their prayers.

I gave my students Bible lessons, homework, and quizzes to ensure that they grew in the knowledge of Christ. By using this method, they received more than a sermon per week. They studied the Bible all week long. I measured their comprehension by checking their written papers. It was like a mini-Bible college.

Less than a month old, our baby son got a nasty eye infection. We did not know where to go for help except to the Lord. When Lydia heard of Andrew's need, she fetched a doctor. The doctor made a house call. She gave us erythromycin and only let us pay $0.25 for her services. The next day, Andrew's eye was better. Praise God!

On the night that Andrew was born in HK, two American missionary friends were tried and charged with breaking Articles 29 and 36 of the PRC's Constitution. At 8:30 pm on November 17, a group of 20 public security officials including a camera crew showed up with a warrant to arrest the missionaries. A thorough search was made of their home for several hours. All contraband was placed in the living room. They were taken to the PSB station at 12:15 am. After several hours of separation and interrogation, the verdict of their crimes was read to them at 6:15 am on November 18. Article 29 deals with smuggling religious material into the PRC and illegally recruiting new religious believers. Article 36 states that religious bodies and affairs are not to be under foreign domination. They were given until November 20 to leave the PRC. One of the women was told that she could not return for three years because this was her second arrest. These ladies were negotiating a contract to start a computer and English language school. Most of their time, however, was used for evangelism and discipleship.

Mr. Liu knew that our Bible study group met on Wednesday evening. Rather than confront me directly about it, and lose me as a teacher, he came to our apartment on Wednesday evenings to visit so that I could not leave. He asked me many questions, but by the grace of God, I evaded divulging info that could be used against my students.

Last Wednesday, I managed to leave the discipleship meeting before he showed up. I was sick. I told my SCAU students that I could only teach for 90-minutes. The Lord protected us that evening. Scarcely had we vacated the meeting room when Mr. Cha pushed open the door and entered in. Mr. Cha asked my friend Constant, "Did you have a guest tonight?" Mr. Cha saw song sheets on the table and picked one up and looked at it. He yelled at Constant, "This is nonsense!" Next, he looked through the books on the bookshelf until he found a Bible. "Do you read this?" he asked. He left the room angerly.

The week after this incident, Mr. Cha moved next door to Constant's dorm room. Constant's father and brother were persecuted during the Cultural Revolution of the 1960's. Constant told me that he was denied a promotion due to his lack of zeal for communism and because of his family history. He only earned $20 per month, but he was generous. He rode his bike with me each week to the Zhongshan University Bible meeting.

The Lord blessed Constant. His mother went to the hospital emergency room due to excessive bleeding. They sent her home because they could not help her. However, after we prayed to Jesus, Her blood flow stopped. She was healed. Everyone who heard about this miracle was amazed.

Another miracle that happened during December was that I brought 40 pounds of Gospel tracts into the PRC safely. A Chinese immigration officer passed his hand right over the area where the tracts were hidden in the bag. He did not detect them. Praise the Lord!

~ Chapter 6 ~
Called to Preach the Gospel (1989)

My relationship with the leaders at SCAU broke down.
They were against me. They spied on me. They expressed anger
at me. Persecution of Christians was on the rise in the city.

After the Reachout Singers did the concerts in November,
Mr. Liu and his comrades frequently visited me. They asked
similar questions during each visit: "Where have you been?"
"What did you do there?" They asked questions to intimidate me.

Like most teachers, we lived in a walled complex. The
entrance to our quarters was monitored by two elderly men. These
men questioned our visitors. They asked them, "What do you do
when you visit him?" The students who became friends with us
were harassed by Mr. Liu and Mr. Cha.

Mr. Liu asked us seven times if he could take Grace to his
home. He said, "My son likes to play with children." When I
asked him old his son was, he replied, "30 years old." Ms. Zhou
urged us relentlessly to let Grace come with her to her school.
Once, she picked up Grace and started to walk away with her. We
insisted "no" and took her back. When I took Grace by Ms.
Zhou's primary school, I found that her students were red
pioneers. Communist loyalist! I told Ms. Zhou to desist from
trying to take our daughter to her school. Finally, she backed off.

After that, Ms. Zhou sent one of her students named Holly
to play with Grace. Holly visited on Sundays while I was teaching

the Bible at Zhongshan University. On two occasions, Holly wore a special ring-shaped collar around her neck. It looked very odd. At one point, Holly gulped and searched inside her shirt as though something had fallen from her collar. When Sherry left the living room to tend baby Andrew in the bedroom, she overheard Holly ask Grace, "Where's your father? Where does he go on Sunday?" Sherry let Holly go that time, but when she showed up a second time wearing this odd collar, and with a friend, and when she started asking Grace questions again after Sherry left the room, Sherry confronted her. "Holly, I think that you are wearing something around your neck that can hear what I am saying." Holly had a guilty look on her face. Her friend shook her head "yes" with a very startled expression. Sherry said, "I want you to tell whoever is sending you or if they are listening to me right now, that we don't appreciate them doing this." The girls stayed a little longer. Before they left, Holly asked Sherry, "Now, that the winter term is over, will you be coming back next term?" They left, but Holly forgot her gloves, so Sherry opened the door of our apartment and called after her. Holly's friend was in the act of tip toeing back towards our door. When she saw Sherry, she ran.

On the last test day, Mr. Sen, the party secretary for SCAU called a meeting for the students and required them to criticize me and the other English teacher whose name was Shaun. This same Mr. Sen told me that he was one out of 30 people that was trained in the former Soviet Union. He was a hardline communist.

An underlying concern that we had was for the safety of our family. We were especially concerned for Grace. She was almost kidnapped once. There was a building being constructed in our compound. Workers wandered about our apartment. The thought occurred to me that the communists might send someone to hurt one of my family members when I was not home. Then, blame the crime on one of the construction workers.

During this stressful season, I made a second trip the US Consulate to calm my concerns about the communist party members at SCAU. When I entered the consulate, I immediately sensed that something was wrong. There was grief on everyone's face. I asked one of the clerks what happened. He told me that someone climbed through the window of an American teacher's apartment and stabbed his 17-year-old daughter to death.

I wanted to pack up and leave as soon as we got back to our apartment, but instead sat up most of the night and prayed. At 10 the next morning, I concluded that it was time to resign my teaching position at SCAU. I submitted to them a 30-day notice according to my contract. Chinese New Year break began January 13 and lasted until February 20. This covered my 30-day requirement of prior notice to end the contact. The first 20-weeks of my contract was over.

Before my students departed for Chinese New Year break, I had the privilege to baptize 14 of them. I also served them communion. Several of them gave me their addresses. I shared their addresses with fellow missionaries to follow up on them.

The believers at Zhongshan University started their own meeting before we left. They continued to do studies that involved answering Bible questions during the meetings. Some in this group had been at meetings where American missionaries were arrested. Others attended Da Ma Zhan Church.

The Da Ma Zhan pastor, Lin Xian Gao, was summoned by the police and ordered to register his church with the government. This was his fourth summons within six months. His church people kept assembling despite the harassment.

Amidst heavy concerns, the Lord blessed us with news that gave us joy. Thanks to God's amazing grace and love, Adam, a medical doctor, led a party member to Jesus. Glory to God!

Constant remained at SCAU. He told me that he scored higher on the TOEFL test than any previous agricultural student in the PRC. Yale University granted him a scholarship to do research in the US.

Lydia and her three daughters took the news of our departure from the university very hard. Lydia could not stop weeping. She said, "When I met you, it was the low time in my life. My husband had just died. But then you came on my husband's (would-be) birthday, and we were so happy. Since we met you, and have known Jesus, it's been like being in the stars. Now, we must say goodbye, we feel very sad." We were speechless. It was like saying goodbye to my mother not knowing if I would see her again. Then, Isaiah 43:4 came to me, and I shared it with her, "Since you are precious and honored in my sight, and because I love you, I will give people in exchange for you, nations in exchange for your life."

I gave Lydia a Bible concordance and Bible dictionary as my farewell gift to her. Sherry gave Lydia her bicycle, vacuum cleaner and spinning machine for drying clothes, but all seemed worthless compared to the love and friendship that she gave us.

Lydia shared a testimony with us before we left. She received a $1,300 court settlement from her husband's crooked business partner. This was an answer to our prayers.

We left the PRC and served with various ministries in HK until July. We did rehab ministry with Jackie Pullinger's ministry. Then, on June 4, 1989, the Communists massacred thousands of students in Tian An Man Square. There was not much we could do for the PRC at that point. We decided to return to the US. We arrived back in the US on July 18, 1989.

~ Chapter 7 ~
Called by the Gospel (1990)

The Lord Jesus graced me with a two-week trip to Taiwan, HK, and the PRC between January 2 – 16. I traveled with Dale Arendt of Advancing Renewal Ministries (ARM), and two pastors from Wisconsin. ARM was founded by Dr. Art Vincent after he retired from teaching at Concordia Seminary St. Louis. He offered to do tax-exempt receipts for supporters of our mission. One of the pastors who traveled with Dale and me was named Jim Buckman. Jim had the privilege of sharing the Gospel with 800 students. 40 of those students surrendered their lives to Christ.

While in Taiwan from January 2 – 13, I ministered in five churches, at Christ's college, at the Formosa Plastic Company, as well as to one bereaved widow and her children. I distributed Gospel tracts in public places. I prayed with and counseled more than 40 people. I visited two seminaries, two Bible colleges and the Taiwan YFC headquarters. I was offered three jobs while in Taiwan: Teaching English at Christ's College, Assisting the Director of Taiwan YFC and pastoring a church whose pastor died four months earlier.

On January 13, I was offered a position to teach Greek and Evangelism at the China Missionary Seminary in HK. RCC offered to sponsor a work visa for me. The Lord led me to act on RCC's offer because with RCC I would focus on evangelism and discipleship in a church setting.

During my trip to HK, I visited with Happy, Miew Tsang and Pak Kai. These teens had attended Sherry's Bible study when we lived in Yau Ma Tei. I visited with missionary Patricia Harmon whose son had recently passed away from a heart attack.

While in Guangzhou City, the Lord graced me to read the Bible with, pray with and worship the Lord with Lydia and two of her three daughters. Lydia allowed me to use her bicycle to pedal to South China Agricultural University. I visited a student there. I was blessed to find that my former student had named his newborn son after me: Mark An Shen. He and other friends greeted me with joy. Many times, my face became warm, and my eyes wet because of my joy to be with them.

The PRC's production was cut by 80% due to countries not buying their products after the Tian An Men massacre. Some workers either received no pay or only 25% of their pay. Large five-star hotels were only 30% occupied. The government invested 25-40% of people's salaries into bonds to survive the economic downturn. Workers were restless. People were afraid to wear jewelry in public due to the crime level. The military was on full alert. Students who participated in the Peaceful Revolution movement were exiled to work on farms, in factories and to serve in the military. Three Christians were arrested for transferring Bibles from foreigners to local Christians. Many hoped that the Communist Party would be overthrown as it was in East Europe.

The day after I returned from the Orient, Larry Sauvageot, the Accelerated Christian Education (A.C.E.) Director of

International Affairs called me and asked if we could pioneer a school in HK. I asked Larry if I could operate this school in conjunction with my work for RCC and he said yes. Missionaries with RCC wanted a school for their children.

This month, I sent 20 copies of my Evangelism Manual to a Pastor Vincente Hernando. He was training disciples in the mountain villages of the Philippines. We met his wife, Mirasol, when she was serving as a maid in HK.

Sherry home-schooled Grace and Glory. Grace did well on her tests. Sherry taught our daughters to read, write, count, and memorize Bible verses.

During February, we did China presentations at the Bible and Literacy League in Hillsboro, MO, and at Trinity Lutheran Church in LaPorte, IN. Though circumstances looked bleak for us to serve in the PRC again, I trusted the Lord to make a way for us. I went with forward with plans to return.

Fellow missionary to the PRC Steve Robinson reported to me that someone from his former university informed on him. The communists watched him closely. Steve was also diagnosed with heart disease. He dealt with fear, loneliness, and temptations, yet continued to preach the Gospel.

RCC applied for visas for us to work with them. We received our work visas to reside in HK on June 11, 1990. The next step was to raise our monthly support to $1,000 per month, and to raise money to buy our airline tickets.

During our time in the US, I served a group of Taiwanese believers. I helped Dr. Young Yang apply for 501©3 status to officially become the Chinese Christian Fellowship Assembly. The West County Assemblies of God Church let them use their facility free of charge for a meeting place. Our first official meeting as a church took place on April 15, 1990, which just happened to be Resurrection Day. I served temporarily as pastor. Young served as head elder. The Lord provided us a pianist and a worship leader. Young interpreted for me. Young and I had visited homes of people during the months leading up to this event. We also did Gospel tract distribution in public places. For example, at the end of a memorial service at the University of Missouri – St. Louis, for the victims of the Tiananmen Square massacre, we distributed tracts. The people were sad. No one refused our literature.

Dr. Yang and I developed doctrinal statements for this congregation using Luther's Catechism, the Westminster Confessions, the Heidelberg Confessions, and the Methodists doctrine in a book entitled, "The Way." We added statements about gifts of the Holy Spirit and the importance of personal evangelism, world missions and helping the poor. The Lord was our source of strength and wisdom.

Mrs. Shei from this congregation shared a testimony with us. She told us, "My friend told me that my face is shining since I started attending the fellowship." After she received the Holy Spirit, she preferred to read the Bible over watching TV. She read the Bible for two hours per night. She prayed one night for an hour and said that it seemed like only 5-minutes had passed by.

We received news that the HK government had opened its 11 Vietnamese refugee camps up to missionaries of RCC. They poured 28,000 Vietnamese Bibles into the camps. They flooded the camps with 20,000 Christian coloring books.

Next, we received news that Pastor Vincente and Mira were blessed with 170 converts in the Philippines. They evangelized four villages. They reported to me that they used the Evangelism Manual that I composed while at YFC to teach five students evangelism techniques.

Jesus led neighborhood people and children to our door in Fenton, Missouri. Grace and Glory taught the children about the Lord. They taught them to pray and to sing to Jesus.

After reading Psalm 37:7-11, I asked the Lord to take away from us the moth that consumes. Immediately after this prayer, I removed an ugly moth from outside our apartment door. A few days later, on August 3, our car sold in Indiana for $1,500. My brother drove us back home to Fenton in time for me to attend a Bible study at the Chinese Church. When that Bible study ended, a Chinese lady gave me a check for $1,000. In addition to this $2,500, I received my paycheck from the nursing home and several checks from donors in the mail. The result of August 3 was that we had enough money to purchase our airline tickets to HK. Plus, we had $1,600 cash to take with us.

I was happy on August 3. I bowed my knees with my face to the floor. I thanked the Lord for His lovingkindness! I thanked God for the gift of faith that He gave to me. We had airline tickets to leave St. Louis on September 1 at 9:05 am and arrive in HK on September 2 at 10:50 pm. Blessed be the Name of the Lord!

On August 10, we received letters from missionary friends who worked with 55,000 Vietnamese refugees in HK. They distributed 30,000 Gospels of Mark, 30,000 Gospel tracts, 30,000 pens with "Jesus loves you" printed on them, and 15,000 boxes of crayons along with 15,000 coloring books based on the Gospel of Mark. They distributed 5,000 Vietnamese Bibles. They provided vitamins to nursing mothers. They reported an average of 20 new believers per week.

When we arrived back in HK, our good friend Anne Hepburn met us at the airport at 11:30 pm. Two days later, she gave Grace and Glory dolls that had bathtubs with water releasing showerheads and faucets. She also gave Andrew a toy. They enjoyed the toys. Anne's assistant, Dak Ming, read Bible stories to them while we purchased children's Bible story books and a song book to take to our friends in the PRC.

We praised God for an all-furnished apartment in Sheung Shui. We took over the $361 rental payments for Wendell and Daisy Martin while they were on furlough in America. This apartment was just a 5-minute train ride to the border of the PRC.

We discovered that Jesus transformed Happy. She had Christian friends. She asked us to pray for her unsaved friends.

112

I continued to do evangelism work on the streets of HK. This was what God placed on my heart to do. Glory to God!

When I met with the Guangzhou Christians, two testified of how the Lord spared them from danger and loss. One sister had a robber flee from her as she prayed to Jesus. Another student had flood waters recede from his house as he prayed to Jesus.

While we were in the States, Lydia hosted two American missionaries, one British missionary family and one Filipino missionary couple. These missionaries brought her top-quality Bible study materials, Christian music tapes and Scripture verses to hang on her walls. Mitz and Rebecca, two Chinese believers, studied the Bible with Lydia and her daughters on a regular basis.

The Guangzhou Christian Fellowship continued to meet twice per week while we were in the US. Mandy Yu was called twice by the PSB and told to report to their office for questioning. Her exact words were, "I really hate this. Please pray for me. Every time they call me, I want to tell them I am too busy or tomorrow, but I have no choice. I really hate it." She shared the Gospel with many. Several had converted.

Chinese Christians estimated that couriers had transported over three million Bibles into the PRC during the last 10 years. Most of these Bibles were transported on the backs of short-term missionaries. Such grace! For example, on one occasion when I carried Bibles across the border, the man watching the x-ray screen left his post and my bag went through.

Happy helped Sherry in various ways. She helped Sherry to teach three to five-year-old children their Sunday school lessons. She brought her friend Suet Hong to visit with Sherry. She and Suet Hong helped Sherry to purchase food at the market and to cook Chinese-style meals. They usually brought little gifts for our children. They helped Sherry to learn Cantonese while she helped them to improve their English-speaking skills.

I preached on a weekly basis at a Vietnamese refugee camp. They requested Bibles and prayer. A man whose English name was Jim asked for prayer for his wife whose English name was Spring. Spring had digestive problems. She was four months pregnant. She had been back and forth to the hospital often.

The refugees slept on sheets of plywood inside large army style tents. They only had thin sheets to divide one family's living area from another's. They stored their few belongings in cardboard boxes. They had no electricity. Several tents worth of people shared one shower and toilet facility.

The Guangzhou Christians contributed $39 towards the purchase of diapers and clothes for the Vietnamese babies in HK. $39 was a substantial because the average person's monthly wage was $35. The average monthly wage in the US during 1990 was $4,183. It was as if they had given nearly $4,200 to missions.

Sherry composed a slide presentation of the refugee ministry for RCC's congregation. After the presentation, she sang the song, "A Tender Heart" by 2nd Chapter of Acts. She made an appeal for diaper and baby clothe donations. An average of nine babies were born per day. The babies lacked diapers and clothes. Winter was fast approaching. She asked the people, "What if those were our children and we had no means to help them? The same hands that formed our children, formed theirs." Praise God! The people donated $193. Combined with the money from the Guangzhou Christians there was $232.

580 children still lacked shoes. Many others lacked warm clothes. John and Francine Allen, directors of RCC's Vietnamese ministry, used Sherry's slide presentation to challenge people in the US to give to the cause as well.

We purchased the following items for Vietnamese children: 20 pairs of shoes, 332 cloth diapers, 90 pairs of socks, 80 plastic baby pants, 120 diaper pins, 11 pants, 22 complete baby outfits and 2 large tubes of Desitin cream for diaper rash. We purchased most of the items in Guangzhou where the cost was less than in HK. For example, a pair of shoes for a two-year-old was 0.81¢. Fur lined children's boots were $1.66. A dozen cloth diapers were $3.50. 40 pairs of baby booties were $11.93. 50 pairs of older children's socks were $22.12.

Two weeks ago, Sherry taught a Bible lesson to over 100 Vietnamese children. Afterwards, about a third of the children prayed and professed faith in Jesus. On Wednesday, I spoke to over 100 Vietnamese refugees on the meaning of water baptism. Afterwards, four missionaries, one HK minister and I baptized 97.

Jim and Spring, mentioned earlier, shared a testimony with me. Jim said, "My wife has not been sick since you prayed for her. It is really amazing." God's grace and love is amazing.

After much prayer for Mandy, the PSB stopped harassing her. God changed the political climate via prayer. We should always pray for those who experience persecution.

Jesus healed Fang Na, the mother of Lily, of a long-term stomach disorder. Praise the Lord! She still needed joy instead of sorrow. She had lost her husband when Lily was two years old. He was persecuted by the government. He became depressed. He died of cancer afterwards. Lily's mother was also persecuted. People avoided her. So, on top of physical healing, she needed healing of depression as well.

We relocated our meeting place because a communist official moved into the neighboring apartment. The new location was not ideal either. Due to the thinness of the walls between the apartments, the believers kept a radio playing to cover the noise of our singing, praying, and speaking. They feared being arrested. I had 26 names and addresses of people to invite to our meetings but waited until we located a safer meeting place.

Despite opposition, the Christians wanted more Bible teaching and more Bible literature. They wanted the Lord to build His Church. They did not want me to stop teaching them. At one meeting, the Holy Spirit baptized four of them. They spoke in tongues. He set one woman free from oppression.

During the last two months, Bible couriers moved more than 70 bags of Bibles into the hands of mainland Chinese. The Lord did miracles. The entrance of God's Word gives light. Light came to the PRC!

10 Christians from Christian Life Center of California helped me to distribute 70 cases of Chinese Bibles and 3,000 Gospel tracts in Macau. In some places, people lined up to receive the free Bibles and tracts. Praise the Lord!

22 Singaporeans Christians did personal witnessing with me at two Chinese temples in HK. Six people professed faith in Christ. Others gave us their names and addresses because they wanted to know more about Christ.

Recently, I met an Australian missionary who spent time in China back in the 1940's. He rode horseback. He slept on the ground while wild tigers could be heard growling in the distance. He hardly ever received letters. He did not receive news of his brother's death until a year after it happened.

I am glad that missionaries who are treated as nothing in this life, are highly esteemed in the Kingdom of God. All who forsake the ambition to be rich and to be great for the sake of being close to Jesus will receive their desire. JESUS!

At age six, Grace was a delightful conversationalist. I enjoyed her so much. She reasoned with me. Grace trusted God. A beautiful example of this is when God dissolved her extreme fear of dogs about two weeks ago. Sherry wrote, "Grace, Glory and I were walking down a path where no dogs live and then, there were two dogs directly on the narrow path before us. Andrew was in the stroller. Grace was alarmed. However, I am certain that what took place next was a miracle. She did not scream frantically as usual even though the closest dog had moved to her side of the narrow path. The dogs were mutts. They were the size of collies. The Holy Spirit reminded me of our past conversations. As we walked slowly, I asked Grace, "Did God make that dog?" She answered, "Yes." I asked her, "Can God control that dog?" She answered, "Yes." I quickly reminded her how God made all things with His fingers and that she is more valuable to Him than any animal. Also, that if she called on the Name of Jesus, then, He would hear her. So, she began saying, "Jesus is Lord." Glory asked if we could sing the song, "Oh the blood of Jesus" while we walked by the dogs. This situation may seem silly, but to Grace it was a serious attack on her life. As we drew closer, the two dogs moved to the side and watched us pass by. After we passed by, they moved back to the middle of the path. Since that time, Grace never asked me, "Can we not go the dog's way?" We also have passed many dogs and cats since then without her screaming and complaining, God answered the prayers of many brothers and sisters in Christ who knew about Grace's "extreme fear" and prayed for her.

Grace was happy to live in HK but wanted to visit the US to see her Grandpa, Grandma, cousins Josiah, Christopher, and Jacob. She also wanted to see Mrs. Donna her favorite Sunday school teacher at Life Christian Center. Glory loved to sing praises to Jesus. She seemingly had a song on her lips all the while she was awake. She was not timid. People told me she was bold. Glory was loving. She gave us many hugs and kisses. She played with Andrew while I taught Grace. She was motherly towards him. Andrew had a special love for Glory.

On December 6, Glory stood on the arm of the sofa and supported her weight on a high stool. This was at the foot of our concrete stairs. Mark was setting the table. I was preparing a meal for missionary friends. Suddenly, the stool fell over and so did Glory. Her face hit the hard step. The impact sounded terrible. She had a huge scratch and bruise just a half inch from her eye. We rebuked the devil. I could only believe that Glory's Heavenly Father would quickly restore her.

Mark took her to the hospital while I waited for our guests to arrive. We had no way to contact them. When the three families arrived, they began interceding for Glory. Two x-rays looked good! No concussion! No cracked bones! Glory to God!

After she returned from the hospital, Glory was chipper. I asked Mark what kind of pain medicine she received. She was so care-free and experiencing no pain. Mark said, "Oh, she has not had pain medicine yet." The day after this incident, Glory wanted to bounce around. She said that only the surface of her face hurt.

Andrew was two-years old. He learned new words daily. He expressed his thoughts cleverly and humorously. He was very delightful. He liked to sing "Happy-doo". It was a song he made-up. He walked with a skip. He loved Glory so much that anytime he received a snack, he asked for one for Glory too. Sometimes, he sat up in the night and called, "Gory". If I showed him where she was and told him she was sleeping, he was happy to go back to sleep. He kept us on our toes. He was courageous, independent, and unpredictable. Most of his activities involved making messes.

During December, Sherry, the children, and other volunteers from RCC did a Christmas outreach to the orphans of St. Christopher's Home in HK. They caroled, shared Scriptures, visited with them and gave them clothes, cakes and cookies. It was a wonderful time for everyone involved.

RCC asked me to take charge of their Vietnamese ministry from December 10, 1990 – January 12, 1991. Directors John and Francine Allen were on furlough in the US. I worked day and night, and sometimes half-way into the night to keep up with the logistics. I cancelled my Guangzhou trips for two weeks.

Right after the directors departed, the refugee camp's security officials threatened to stop our Saturday worship services. The attendance at our meetings grew at an incredible rate. During September, there was just a handful of attendees. By December, we had nearly 900 attendees per week. Security officials said that we could no longer invite refugees from all four sections of the camp into one place. We either had to limit the number of attendees per meeting or stop the meetings. After prayer, the Lord showed us to divide the attendees up according to sections where they lived. Going forward, we did four meetings simultaneously on Saturdays instead of one large meeting. This

120

way, the refugees remained in their assigned sections, and were less threatening to the guards. This proposal was approved. We recruited additional missionaries to help. We grew to 35 volunteers per week. The guards cancelled our mid-week Bible study services, but at least, we were not banned from the camp. The Shek Kong UNHCR Camp had over 7,000 refugees.

RCC Vietnamese Ministries provided 400 hard-boiled eggs per week to the refugees. Teachers taught them English. We provided them with transportation and drivers between Monday and Friday for checkups at the hospital and for marriage ceremonies at the courthouse. Local churches donated 72,000 pairs of shoes, 75 jackets and 13 van loads of clothing. A Gospel tract was designed and printed in Vietnamese. More than a 1,000 hard-cover Vietnamese Bibles were distributed. More than 2,000 toys were distributed. Candies and chocolates were given to the children. 287 converts were baptized.

Sherry contributed a hand-colored 14-foot mural of the Christmas story for the refugees. It was amazing what God did. God brought His kingdom to earth through us.

As we humbled ourselves before the Lord and repented of our sins, He came to us and lifted us up. The Spirit led me to start my prayers with repentance. Then, the Spirit led me to worship the Lord with songs of praise and love for Him. I read and studied His Word. As He built my confidence in His love and in His power, then, I petitioned Him on behalf of the people of the PRC, HK, the US, and other countries as time permitted. The Spirit led me to pray over my to-do list. The days when I took time to meet with Jesus like this were always better than the other days. I am not worthy of Jesus, but I am thankful that He is my Lord and Savior. He listened to me as I mentioned those I love before Him.

One the greatest ways to express our love to Jesus is to preach the Gospel. Jesus paid such a terrible and painful price to wash away our sins. If the Gospel is not preached and unbelievers remain lost, His great sacrifice remains hidden. Praise the Lord that He gives His Holy Spirit to be with us. It is wonderful to preach the Gospel out of conviction and revelation given by the Holy Spirit, and not out of a mechanical head knowledge only.

~ Chapter 8 ~
Called by the Gospel (1991)

Sherry and the children joined me on their second trip to Guangzhou this month. Most of our Bibles were confiscated this time. One Greek-Chinese-English New Testament worth $33, two worship tapes, and a few small Bible booklets made it through. During the confiscation process, two guards took me to a small room to search, question and scold me. Two female guards took Sherry to another room to do the same to her. At first, they were not going to let Sherry keep the children with her, but she adamantly refused to be separated from them. So, they permitted the children to remain with her.

After the border ordeal, we boarded a train to Guangzhou. The center aisle of the train car was packed with people. The air was stuffy. People with dirty hands were touching our children's faces. In Guangzhou, black market con artists followed us down a sidewalk trying to strike a "deal" with us. Beggars pleaded with us for money. We bought fruit to give to them. We supplemented the fruit with Gospel tracts. It was no longer safe to travel the street at night. Three girls from our fellowship barely escaped being attacked by men this month.

When we reached the house church, the believers were happy and encouraged to see Sherry and the children. The Lord gave us specific Scriptures to share with them. The Lord blessed us with love for one another.

Lydia was especially happy to see Sherry and the children. Lydia was sick. She was experiencing heart palpitations. A doctor advised her to stop working and to check-in at the hospital. She stayed at home, read her Bible, and prayed for others. We prayed for her. She asked us to pray for her daughter Mercy. Mercy served at a house church in Beijing. She lived with her non-Christian uncle and aunt. This concerned Lydia.

Bill and Louise taught me Cantonese. During my last lesson, I learned how to use a Chinese dictionary. The Chinese dictionary uses a system of pen-strokes for reference. Some curvy strokes are still only one stroke because the pen never leaves the paper when drawing them. Other characters have as many as 30 strokes. At first, it seemed complicated, but after I learned the root characters, it was not difficult to discern how a complexed character was just a combination of root characters placed together. Grace and Glory practiced writing the characters with me. I learned 100 characters. Bill and Louise refused payment for the lessons. They were answers to people's prayers for me.

Our need for an apartment was urgent. We needed to vacate our current apartment by February 4. We were certain our Heavenly Father would help us. We had received gifts of furniture and household items. We praised the Lord in advance for what He was about to do.

Just one week before we needed to vacate our apartment, the Lord provided us a two-bedroom apartment with 580 square feet of space in Fanling Wai for $254 per month. We did not have to pay the standard middle-man's fee of one month's rent. We only paid a month and half's deposit fee instead of the standard two-month's rent deposit fee. Other missionaries rented apartments in this village. A hospital was next door to the village. Every kind of needed shop was within a 20-minutes walking distance. Many bus stops were close by. The village had a playground and a small park. The border of the PRC was 30-minutes from our front door. We had furniture and appliances.

Two weeks ago, I prayed for Trinh Dam Thuc's wife. She left Vietnam two-months ago by boat. He had not heard from her. Sometimes sailors rescued these boat women only to abuse them and dump them overboard to drown. Mr. Trinh was depressed. The Holy Spirit led me to pray specifically that the Lord would bring her to the Shek Kong Refugee Camp, security section B and bring her soon. Well, last Saturday, Mrs. Trinh Bac Sieu was in section B. When the invitation was given for unbelievers to repent and believe in Christ, she was the first one to come forward. Mr. Trinh told me that her boat had landed on a small uninhabited island that lacked food. After she set back out to sea, a big wind came and blew her straight to HK. Mr. Trinh told this testimony to the entire congregation.

The UNHCR guaranteed community huts to us in which to meet each week, but some security guards and refugees troubled us. The Buddhists complained to the camp directors about us. The directors cancelled our midweek services. Thankfully, we were permitted to hold Bible studies on Saturday mornings.

After John and Francine Allen returned from the US, they resumed their roles as directors. I was assigned to co-pastor section B of this camp. I was happy for the opportunity.

The Lord led two pastors from the St. Louis area, one from Ohio, one from Minnesota and me to bring Bibles into the PRC. The believers received a bookshelf worth of Christian leadership materials. They were grateful for these resources.

Sister Sharon translated the Chinese Christian Fellowship Assembly's Statements of Faith from English into Chinese. I sent a copy to the Taiwanese Church in St. Louis. I hand delivered copies of it to the believers in Guangzhou. I drafted these statements using the Bible and several protestant catechisms. Dr. Young Yang, Jim Spencer and Ron and Beth Wesley helped me to edit and improve the drafts. Sharon also translated a document that I composed from the Book of Proverbs. I distributed it to the believers in the PRC.

Marsha Harmon of Open-Heart Evangelistic Association asked us to record a three to four-minute cassette tape of our missionary testimony. It was aired on KIRL on a Friday evening between 7:45-8:00 pm. KIRL broadcasts in St. Louis.

RCC had me lead Wednesday evening English classes. The first term began on March 6 and lasted 10 weeks. I developed curriculum for three levels of English language instruction. I recruited teachers from among the missionaries. This was an effort to attract people to Christ.

Bill and Louise taught me how to read the Chinese Bible. We started with John's Gospel. They had me read the Chinese characters out loud in Cantonese. They had more faith in me than I had in myself. I thanked God for them.

Three Christians from RCC helped me to do a question-and-answer discussion with the Guangzhou disciples on how to follow-up new converts. Evangelist David Feltz shared a powerful message with them. He had evangelized in 48 countries. Last year, by God's grace, he spearheaded a movement to bring 250,000 Bibles into the USSR.

Before our March 11 meeting began, I experienced a dream twice. As I prayed, the dream came to me again. Suddenly, I understood that the Lord wanted me to speak on the gift of discerning spirits and to warn the flock against lying spirits that would lead them from Christ. As I began sharing, they looked at each other with amazement and smiles. So, I asked, "Matyeh?" (What?) They replied, "We were talking about this topic before you arrived. Glory to God! Thank You Holy Spirit!

Bill and Louise printed a brochure that I designed to introduce people to the Chinese Christian Fellowship Assembly. They used their Chinese computer. I mailed it to the Taiwanese believers in St. Louis. I also took copies of it to the believers in Guangzhou. This way, they could formulate their own brochure.

We visited with Lydia for two nights. She had Scripture posters on all her walls and one on her entrance door that stated, "Jesus... said, 'I am the light of the world. Whoever follows Me

will never walk in darkness but will have the light of life.'"
Sherry and the children enjoyed the visit. Lydia updated us on her
family's situation. Afterwards, we shared Scripture with them.
We prayed for them. Lydia was concerned for her daughter
Mercy. She was doing church work in Beijing. Her other daughter
Persis was the executive secretary to the president of her
company. She witnessed to him. He attended church with her. He
asked her questions about God. Persis hoped to lead him to Christ.

Satan moved the PRC's leaders to oppress their people.
They sent some to labor camps. Beat others. Imprisoned still
more. Pictures of Chairman Mao were pasted in public places.
Some worshipped Mao as though he were a god. One artist
produced a record entitled, "Songs of the Revolution" that
featured Mao's favorite songs. Mao and his regime slaughtered
perhaps as many as 10 million people including many Christians.

Six out of Sherry's ten Sunday school students sang four
songs on Sunday morning. They sang, "Turn it over to Jesus and
you will smile the rest of the day." As we turned our concerns
over to Jesus, He helped us to travel light.

Two men believed in Jesus at the Vietnamese fellowship.
We had 24 believers in Section B to baptize. God blessed Jim and
Spring with a healthy baby boy. Another brother testified how
faith in Christ helped him to endure hardships. Two teenage girls
asked for prayer. We had over 60 people in the fellowship.

During June, 111 Vietnamese people arrived on one boat.
The closest Vietnamese city to HK was 800 miles away by sea.

5,500 people arrived during the first five months of 1991 compared to 6,598 that arrived during the entire year of 1990. 53,000 refugees lived in HK's 11 refugee camps. Some refugees had waited five years for a country to accept them.

In May, our Shek Kong congregation was transferred to the Tai A Chau Camp. I was not allowed to enter Tai A Chau, but there was a group of refugees at High Island Camp that wanted me to serve them. I opted to ask my pastoral assistant Steve Robinson to take the lead position in the High Island ministry. I wanted to improve my Chinese. Steve continued to assist me with the ministry in Guangzhou. I assisted him at High Island Camp.

Nine Vietnamese professed faith in Christ at the High Island Camp during May. Our average attendance was 50 refugees per week. I felt blessed to be a part of this ministry.

RCMI sent six people to Xinjiang Province. They located a church there. They gave them 12 cases of Bibles. The church was located among the Uygur people. 50 Christians attended the services. There were seven million Uygur people and previously to this trip there was no known church among them.

One of the Guangzhou Christians handed a note to me. He wrote, "Dear Teacher Mark: I appreciate we have a teacher from God, because you care for each of us fairly, and make God our first love, and highest position at all times, and show us an example by faith. Thank You Lord for taking care of us."

Additionally, a group of African medical and agricultural students asked me to find someone to teach them how to minister

129

to the Chinese. I felt unable to take on another ministry, so I referred them to Pastor Ken Knosp. I led Ken to the first meeting. There were 20 countries of Africa represented at the meeting. Prior to bringing Ken, I had arranged speakers twice for this group. The Lord did a notable miracle via a visiting evangelist. A medical doctor who had a broken leg was totally healed. Knowing that he was healed, he sawed off his cast and ran up and down the dormitory stairs. An unbelieving African saw this miracle and asked the visiting evangelist to lead him to Christ. The doctor walked around totally healed.

Sherry let our Fanling apartment be a venue for HK teens to eat and to pray together. We also shared Scriptures one with another. We prayed for Pak Kai to believe in Jesus. We prayed for the mother of Annie Yun. Her mother lived in fear.

During July, Happy became a group leader at RCC's teen fellowship. She co-led singing during RCC's Sunday morning worship service. Happy visited us regularly. She usually invited others to come with her. She brought leaders from the youth group to our home. We prayed for them.

Happy invited us to visit her sick grandmother. Her grandma was in the Buddhist Hospital. She wanted us to witness to her grandma and to pray for her. Happy spent entire days at the hospital with her grandmother to provide her company and to share the Gospel with her. Her grandmother was 82 years old and had not believed in the Lord yet.

A few months ago, Happy invited a 16-year-old girl named Annie to our home. Annie visited us on a regular basis. She enjoyed playing with our children and talking about Jesus with us. One Sunday, Annie contemplated suicide because of mistreatment from her family. We prayed for her and shared Scriptures with her. The next week, she was happy because she had shared with a man how Jesus gave her eternal life. This man had just lost his wife. He was very grateful to hear her testimony. The next week, she came to us quiet and sad. Her father had beat and scratched her. He was an alcoholic. Sherry told Annie to consider our home a place of refuge. Annie and Happy have stayed at our home with Sherry and the children while I was in the PRC. Annie visited often for prayer, counseling and to play with Grace, Glory and Andrew. Her ability to speak English was limited. A good opportunity for us to learn Cantonese!

On Saturday, Sherry began six weeks of Vacation Bible School lessons for three to eleven-year-olds. The children mostly spoke Cantonese. Peggy Knosp and Danielle Ho helped her. They did Bible stories, songs, skits, arts, and crafts with the children.

Pastor Dennis asked Sherry to present the Vietnamese ministry to the 50 members of the young adult fellowship by way of song and slide pictures. She did it. After that, the presentation was shown in the US by the directors of the Vietnamese ministry, and in Malaysia by a fellow missionary. Praise the Lord! Jesus, inspired Sherry to do this project. It yielded good results.

131

15 students finished our English classes. One woman, Liza Tang, professed faith in Christ. She attended worship services. Attendance for our next term exceeded 50 students. Our goal was to lead the non-believing students to faith in Christ.

Louise encouraged me to write a testimony in Chinese using 100 characters. At first, I thought she had asked me to do the impossible, but with God's help, I did it. Praise the Lord! I even drafted some simple sentences flawlessly.

The Lord blessed me with a five-month season of not being caught with Bibles by border guards. The Communists made a public declaration this month that they intended to crackdown on crime. One of the crimes they intended to crack down on was foreign intervention in religious affairs.

During August, 40 Vietnamese professed faith in Christ at High Island Camp. We had a baptism service for them. One new believer named Mihn had read his Bible from cover to cover.

During August, the PRC was hit by severe flooding. Millions went hungry and homeless. One Christian sister walked for two weeks to the nearest Christian meeting point to report that their crops were completely wiped out. Their Bibles were destroyed. After giving this report, she fainted due to hunger. She told them that the government was neglecting Christians. No relief was sent to them. This sister was from Anhui Province where there was an estimated five million Christians.

Last week, the Lord graced me to transfer 120 Bibles and 50 Christian books to a pastor. I gave him an offering of $1,300 from the HK Christians. He was very grateful for these gifts.

During September, two students professed faith in Christ at the Guangzhou Fellowship. They had only started attending the previous month. The Lord kept adding to His church.

After eight months of meeting in the home of Lily, we moved our meeting place to an art exhibition center. Her mother became unsettled about us meeting in their apartment. The art exhibition center was good for three weeks-worth of meetings. But three things about the location did not sit well with us. There were Buddhist idols on display. Some Christians did not attend because the location was too far for them. Before the last meeting, an army truck full of soldiers arrived at the center as we arrived. That alarmed us. Later, we found out that an important dignitary from Italy had arrived. The soldiers were assigned to create a perimeter around the area.

Security tightened in Guangzhou during September. Some soldiers carried machine guns as they walked the sidewalks. The Christians started doing larger gatherings when we foreigners were not in around. At stake, was the risk that we would lead PSB agents to the meeting places, and the Christians would be arrested. I did home visitations with new believers to lead their families to Christ. Personal visits rather than large meetings! I typed and copied sermons with Chinese translations to give to them.

On September 7 – 9, Sherry and the children joined me on a trip to Guangzhou to visit the boss of Persis. We shared Scriptures with him and urged him to attend church, to pray and to read his Bible. He was very good to us. He gave us a tour of the shoe factory. I mentioned to him that I preached in a sowing factory in Shenzhen, and at the Formosa Plastic Company in Taiwan. I hoped that he would feel at liberty to allow me to preach to the workers. We met with Lydia and her family twice. We met with the members of the Guangzhou Fellowship.

In HK, Annie Yun's uncle professed faith in Christ. Annie told Sherry that she would not be baptized until God showed her through His Word to do so. Sherry shared with Annie about the Ethiopian Eunuch of Acts 8. He was baptized the moment he believed in Jesus. After that conversation, Annie decided to be baptized during the next baptism service at RCC on October 27. However, even before her baptism, she led a classmate to Christ and bought him a Bible with her own money.

On September 6, a typhoon struck HK. We still held our meeting at High Island Camp. We met under the roof of an open pavilion structure. Both the Holy Spirit and wind were blowing. We had to stand during the entire the meeting because the concrete was too wet sit on. Even so, 50% of the congregation showed up to worship Jesus. Praise God!

On September 13, Steve Robinson and I baptized the majority of 106 converts at High Island Camp. There were two other teams of pastors baptizing converts as well. Praise God!

On September 20, a man professed faith in Christ during the meeting. After we prayed with him, the police ordered us to leave immediately. Refugees had torn pieces of tin from the Quonset huts and formed the tin into knives. Others pulled up metal drain covers and broke them into sharp pieces. Over 100 Vietnamese prepared to fight. As we exited, police in full riot gear entered the camp. They had helmets, shields, clubs, and tear gas guns. As we drove away, we saw a jeep full of soldiers with guns. Most of the people in this camp were war veterans who fled Vietnam for fear of being executed. We prayed for the innocent people that were caught in the middle of this war zone.

On another occasion, we were denied access into the camp because a refugee was murdered. The refugee children witness rapes, fights, and murders. Some have lived at High Island Camp for two years. The population now exceeds 63,000 refugees.

British Prime Minister John Major personally visited High Island Camp this month. Our interpreter got to meet and speak with him. He said the Prime Minister was very touched by the warm welcome of the refugees and by the poor conditions that most of them endured with great patience.

During October, I visited one of my students named Shineng. I had not seen him in over two years. He lived 30-minutes outside the city limits of Guangzhou. Yesterday, Ken Knosp and I went to visit him. The taxi dropped us off a mile too soon at the wrong institution. We started to walk, but the "wrong" institution offered to take us to the "right" institution in their air-

135

conditioned van. We accepted the offer. They dropped us at Shineng's doorstep. My former student was now the director of foreign affairs, and a communist party official. Even so, he was excited to see me. He stopped his work and invited us into his house. We shared the Gospel with him. We told him of God's concern for the poor and oppressed people of Guangzhou. He was very opened hearted. He requested a Bible. He asked us to return on November 11. Our time with him passed quickly. Suddenly, we realized that we had one hour to catch the last train back to HK. We asked if there were buses or taxis available. He replied, "No, impossible. And all our institution's cars are on assignment, or I would give you a ride to the station." I told Shineng how God always provides for us. "God provided the van that brought us to your doorstep. I believe God will provide." As soon as we reached the gate, a taxi pulled up. Shineng exclaimed, "Jesus provided a taxi for you." We laughed and said, "Yes."

Pastor Rick Shelton, his son Joshua and Jack Harris of Life Christian Center in St. Louis helped us carry Bibles into the PRC. We distributed Gospel tracts and a Bible. After that, people passed notes to us requesting more Bibles. One man who received a Bible asked me to explain it to him. I spoke Cantonese to him, and he spoke Mandarin to me. He was from Henan. This went on for two hours. A third man who spoke Cantonese and Mandarin helped us to understand one another. The man believed in Jesus and wrote his profession of faith in Christ on a paper. I still have his note. Praise the Lord!

Sherry was pregnant. Some days, she suffered morning sickness all day long and other days no sickness at all. Perhaps, she would have another boy because this was how she felt when she was pregnant with Andrew. Either way, we would be happy.

Sherry shared the Gospel with a 16-year-old girl named Saan. Saan was Annie's classmate. Saan came from a family of nine. Her parents were alcoholics. Saan's mother attempted to commit suicide last week by slashing her wrists. Her father was physically abusive. Saan professed faith in Christ a week ago. She asked Sherry to keep sharing Jesus with her.

One of my English students named Liza Tang was baptized in November. Annie was also baptized. Glory to God!

Persecution of Christians was on the rise. Mandy had been questioned twice by the PSB. Dr. Adam Wong moved to Fujian Province. Lily and Piper transferred to other fellowships. Jack Tan disappeared. The Guangzhou Fellowship broke up when Lily's mother asked us to find a new meeting place. The new meeting place did not meet their expectations. Mandy continued to meet with some Christians in her home.

After communism collapsed in the USSR, the PRC's communist party became "trigger happy." There were executions in every major city. Recently, 141 criminals were shot at one time in Kunming. The executions were televised in HK. Crowds gathered and watched the execution as though it was a sporting event. Executions took place before spectators in Shenzhen and Guangzhou. A Burmese pastor had his ribs broken and afterwards was hung upside down until he died. He had smuggled books into the PRC to explain to Christians why Marxism was anti-Christian. Some Shanghai Christians were beaten with rods and their pastor was arrested. The pastor's crime was that he took clothes to the flood victims in Anhui Province. He was accused of treason because he gave glory to Jesus and not to the communist party. Beijing made it a crime to listen to unauthorized foreign radio broadcasts. Beijing made it a crime to receive or read books from foreigners. One contact reported that the police were no longer protecting Christians. People could do to them as they wished.

RCMI published a book entitled, "Lilies Among the Thorns." The book contains the testimonies of Chinese Christians. One Christian was buried alive in coffin. He was told that if he rejected Jesus that he would be set free. After six hours, he refused to deny Christ, so they nailed the coffin shut and buried him alive. A 16-year-old girl was placed in a tiny cell for proclaiming Christ. There was nowhere to sit except on the floor and the floor was covered in excrement. She asked the Lord what to do. He gave her the idea to offer to clean up the prison cells. The guards let her do this. As she cleaned, she met prisoners who had not seen anyone for a long time. She shared the Gospel with the prisoners, and many believed in Christ.

An American pastor attended a large meeting in Henan. A Christian had just been released from prison. He shared tales of his sufferings. The Christians began to weep. At first the pastor thought they were crying for the man, but then, he heard the

Christians saying, "Lord, how blessed he is that he can suffer for You. Oh, that You would allow me the same privilege." After this, they began to sing a chorus entitled, "To be a martyr for the Lord." The chorus described how the apostles were martyred that others might be saved.

Pastor Steve Robinson was on furlough, so I preached for him at the High Island Detention Center. I gave a message on being a disciple of Jesus. Then, I asked who wanted to be a disciple of Christ. The whole congregation of 50 people came forward. I prayed for the sick. One man testified that after I prayed for him, his horrible headaches ended. Someone had beaten his head severely. Jesus healed him.

Grace was in second grade and Glory was in kindergarten. Andrew was about to turn three. He wanted to begin school. Sherry learned that she was pregnant with baby number four. We were happily surprised and thankful to God for another child.

On November 8, I had the privilege to lead a citizen of the PRC to freedom. Her husband, former missionaries Robert and Donna Weathersby and a host of prayer warriors had prayed for this miracle since July. The Presbyterian Seminary in Louisville, Kentucky, sponsored her student visa. They gave her a full scholarship. She shared her testimony on November 10 at RCC. Her name was Mei Sheng.

Mei Sheng shared this testimony with us:

My mother studied in a church school, but before she finished or was baptized, the revolution took place. My mother was persecuted for her faith. Mother showed me a school, hospital, and church that Christians had built.

I was taught atheism in the public school. During my third year at the seminary, some western seminary students gave us Gospel tracts and preached the Gospel to the students. This was when I woke up to the fact that the Lord had called me and saved me. I had no way to get a Bible, but the Lord did not forget me.

I graduated and started work. I visited a church. Christians there introduced me to an American. He (Robert) gave me a Bible and taught me God's Word. I believed in Christ. The Lord protected me.

I am a lawyer. All my friends are atheists. They believe in communism. I felt called to preach salvation to them because these are the last days.

I had many difficulties to get a passport. The government keeps pushing Marxism. Many people predicted that I would never get a passport. I asked the Lord to destroy the works of the enemy and show His mighty power to my friends. I was granted the visa. I am happy to be liberated. God's grace is abundant and wonderful! We should worship the Lord!

During December, Sherry shared the Gospel with a young Chinese man named Austin and he immediately professed faith in Christ. He was to have cancer surgery but showed signs of recovery. The operation was delayed. His father and mother professed faith in Christ as well. Ken Knosp led the mother to

Jesus. Many witnessed to the father before he believed. We asked the Lord to heal the tumor in Austin's lung.

I completed seven more weeks of Cantonese study. I prepared to enroll into another seven-week course. Sherry and the children learned from me and from others. As I followed along in the Chinese Bible as I listened to Chinese Bible tapes. I translated a discipleship manual from Chinese into English to learn new vocabulary words. I minimized my time with people who spoke English so that I was forced to converse in Cantonese. I resigned from the Vietnamese ministry on December 6 to focus on ministry to the Chinese. A missionary named Clay McMann replaced me.

The Vietnamese congregation was greatly saddened by my departure. Several of the North Vietnamese Christians started weeping. It was difficult to pull away. It took me a whole hour to say goodbye because they encircled me and did not want me to leave. I had a knot in my heart for a few hours afterwards. I felt so sad and touched by them. Incidentally, two more Vietnamese professed faith in Christ during my last meeting.

Last month, we invited eight of my English class students to eat with us. We shared more about Jesus with them. Wai Man professed faith in Christ.

This month, we shared the Gospel with a mother of five children. They lived in a small tin hut. They had mattresses on the floor for beds. They climbed a hill to use an outhouse for their restroom. The mother and one daughter professed faith in Christ.

On December 19, Andrew had severe gastro-enteritis. He could not hold down food or drink. I took Andrew to the hospital on December 21 at 11 pm. Five hours later, on December 22, at 4 am, he was admitted into the hospital. He was placed on an IV drip. I stayed with Andrew in the hospital for three days. He had a 103 fever and was severely dehydrated. Many people prayed for him. Andrew was discharged on Christmas Eve afternoon.

At 11 pm, on Christmas Eve, I joined 25 of RCC's young people to do an outreach on a busy street corner. Happy sang. Syut Hong distributed Gospel tracts. Annie shared her testimony. Kok Fai, Ah Biu and Chi Ming also shared their testimonies. I preached in Cantonese. The three-hour outreach passed quickly due to the conversations that we enjoyed.

On Christmas Day, missionary friends brought us turkey and pumpkin pie. Relatives sent us Christmas gifts. We enjoyed opening them. We enjoyed being together as a family.

The US government pressured the PRC to halt its cruel treatment of people. The PRC's response was to increase the abuse. Her leaders threatened the US with a decline in good relations. Mao's picture hung in many places. A TV show and record album was produced about Mao. The government encouraged people to read the writings of Marx, Lenin, and Mao Zedong. The PRC accused the US of trying to incite a civil war. The PRC also disliked the fact that the US had set up refugee camps for the Kurdish people in Iraq. We asked people to pray for the oppressed Chinese people, and for the Kurds as well.

The PRC placed people who were loyal to the Han majority in regions that were predominantly populated by minorities. Students complained that they did not want to be separated from their families and relatives. The government restricted people by requiring them to apply for permission to travel before traveling outside their assigned area.

The people resented the one-child per family law. One of our friends, Mary Su, was forced to abort her second child. Some parents abandoned baby girls due to this law. Some parents aborted baby girls when a sonogram revealed the gender.

The South China Morning Post told of a video that the Communists released to its party members. One statement on the video was, "We must strangle the baby of Christianity while it is still in the cradle." The government blamed the collapse of communism in East Europe and in the USSR on Christians.

Sherry watched four-year old Andrew while home-schooling Grace and Glory. Grace and Glory made "A's" and "Bs" on their tests. Grace was in second grade and Glory was in first. Grace was given a BMX bicycle and learned how to ride it without training wheels. Andrew was active and talkative. All was happy and blessed. Then on December 16, they contracted chicken pox. The toys that they received on Christmas Day helped them to pass the time while they waited to be well again. It was the second week of January before they all recovered.

~ Chapter 9 ~
Called by the Gospel (1992)

Mr. Wu and Persis wanted to be married in the sight of God and God's people. Lydia asked Pastor Lamb to say the prayer during the wedding. She asked me to give the blessing. I also gave a brief Bible teaching on the love of God as the best foundation on which to build a marriage. It was a beautiful wedding. We were so privileged to be included on their special day.

My English class students, Wai Wan and his sister Wai Ha, professed faith in Christ. They heard and believed the Gospel in my class. We started a new term January 15. All last term's students returned. Three new students enrolled.

Piper married an Australian and immigrated to Australia. He is a Christian. Linda Pang, Lydia's oldest daughter left the PRC for Australia. She went on a student visa to study English.

We delivered toys, clothes and $65 to Pui Saan's family. We prayed for Pui Saan to get a job in art design. She was a highly gifted artist.

The Guangzhou Fellowship meetings pulled me away from Sherry one night and two days per week. We had no car and only a very small refrigerator which meant Sherry had to take the children with her to the market daily. She hung her grocery bags from the stroller's handles. No car trunk! She carefully controlled the children from running out onto the busy street. She home-schooled the older two. She watched Andrew while doing chores.

Pastor Dennis wrote the following endorsement to our prayer and financial supporters, "I am the pastor of the church that Mark and Sherry Czanderna are working with. They are very active in the church and doing a great work for the Lord. They have done great work in Mainland China and now in Hong Kong are leading many to the Lord. Mark is diligent in studying Cantonese. He will soon be able to start preaching in the language and even start his own church. We are very strong in church planting and encourage all missionaries to aim to start new works. But even now they are very active in evangelism."

I had to make hard choices. For example, to spend time alone studying Chinese characters. I used flash cards as I rode on buses and trains to increase my Chinese vocabulary. I translated Bible materials to learn terms to teach systematic theology and apologetics. I memorized Scriptures in Chinese. I put myself in front of people and started conversations with them about Christ.

During January, we distributed 8,200 Christmas toys to children. We had enough toys leftover to bless a fourth refugee camp. The fourth camp had many children with special needs.

HK and Vietnam reached an agreement to start the repatriation process of returning refugees back to Vietnam. The camps were to be vacated within two to three years. They would be sent back at the rate of 2,000 per month. HK could not keep them indefinitely. Many were under nourished when they arrived. Some had cholera. We hoped that the converts who returned to Vietnam would share the good news of Christ with others.

One Saturday, as we prepared to leave Shek Kong camp, some of the Christians asked us to attend a special meeting the next morning at 8 am. Since Sunday was our one day of rest per week, and the day on which we worshipped God at church, we were reluctant to say yes. But the Holy Spirit led us to say, "Yes."

When we came back the next morning, they wanted us to pray for a woman who was unconscious on her bed. We could not wake her. She had been in this condition for four days without medical attention. We anointed her with oil and prayed for her. We didn't see any improvement. We sat her up and gave her a sip of water. She swallowed. We asked the Christians to have someone stay with her to keep her hydrated and to pray for her.

After we left the camp, the Spirit led John to turnaround. He had an unopened energy drink. He wanted to give it to the woman. When we returned, she was wide awake, alert, smiling and thirsty. A few days later, she was well again. Praise God!

I wrote to Sherry's parents, "We are living at Curtis and Mei Lin's house now in Fanling until February 25. At that time, our new apartment will be ready for us to move in. It is nice. It has two bedrooms."

We were fighting off infections as we continued to serve. Sherry suffered with severe allergy symptoms. Despite her discomfort, she had a group of children ready to sing on Sunday.

Andrew entered the hospital last December. He was there for two weeks. He entered the hospital a second time from February 9 – 15, and for a final stay from February 18 – 22.

During the third stay, the medical staff finally identified his problem. It was shigella. During his earlier hospital stays, Andrew received antibiotic. The antibiotic reduced the symptoms but did not eliminate the illness. After each treatment, the shigella came back stronger than before. During the third stay, the doctor gave him Sceptrin. Andrew's life was saved thanks to God using Louise's father-in-law. Roy Rowland had his physician talk with our physician. He diagnosed what Andrew had and told the HK doctor what to do about it. Andrew recovered quickly after this.

In addition to Andrew's trials, Grace and Glory had the flu with high fever. Sherry's mom came to help us. She had fever for two days. I had fever for one day. I needed a minor surgery that landed me in the hospital for three days. Our greatest concern was for Sherry. She was pregnant. She contracted the shigella and was in the hospital from February 22 – 28. We needed a miracle!

On the day that these trials ended, we had read Psalm 91. She was at the hospital reading Psalm 91 in the night. I was reading Psalm 91 during the early morning hours. When I went to visit Sherry that day, she was waiting in the hallway. She was being released. She was better. As we talked of our experiences, we were surprised to discover how God had led us both to Psalm 91. We praised God for the gift of faith and for the miracle that He had done. Many Christians called us, encouraged us, visited with us, brought us gifts, and prayed for us. April Chan from RCC told us, "The whole church prayed for you."

100,000 northern Chinese came to Guangzhou per day to look for work. The train station was swamped with poor people sleeping and sitting everywhere. Crime ran rampant.

At High Island camp, there were reports of murders and of domestic violence. I prayed for one man who wept hysterically. His brother, sister-in-law, niece, and nephew were killed in a fire set by an arsonist.

On March 26, doctors confirmed that Sherry no longer had shigella. She was better. I stayed at home more. We rested and read biographies of missionaries together.

On March 28, two major prayer requests were answered. Fang Na and her daughter Lily moved from Guangzhou to a place God prepared for them. Christians from another city cared for them. They committed to help Lily deliver her baby. If she had stayed in Guangzhou, it was certain that the government would have forced her to abort her baby. The government asked Fang Na to move out of her apartment. The Lord provided a new apartment for her. Missionary Ron Paul Bordelon gave me $12.50 to give to her. That was the exact amount the movers charged her.

Leaders of RCC offered to pay for weekly expenses connected to my ministry in Guangzhou. Sherry and I had been financing this ministry to the tune of a $100 per week. As the ministry grew, so did our cost. The Lord provided!

Psalm 119:130 says, "The entrance of Your words gives light; it gives understanding to the simple." Spreading the Word of God to people was our way to bring light to the dark places of

148

the earth. Sherry promoted Scripture memorization among Chinese, Korean, and Vietnamese children. Our children and others have memorized entire chapters of Scripture. Glory to God!

On March 29, Pastor Dennis returned from a two-week trip to Russia and Ukraine. Though he returned to HK at 2 am, he provided us a wonderful message during the Sunday worship service. He reported that one of his travelling partners, Pastor Moses Vegh, met the president of the Commonwealth of Independent States (CIS), Mr. Boris Yeltsin. Yeltsin claimed to be a believer in Jesus Christ. Yeltsin urged Vegh to bring as many Gospel teams as he could to the CIS to go into schools, hospitals, and churches. Yeltsin said, "Only God can save Russia. Russia needs the Gospel."

Atheism made a nation with 7,000 years of culture and history into a beggar nation. A stadium with a seating capacity of 4,200 could be rented for just over $1,000 per month. The average monthly income was between $10-25.

Pastor Dennis attended a meeting with over 1,000 Russians. This meeting was held inside a large hotel in Moscow. The Christians were poor yet full of joy. They sang and danced to the Lord. Next to the meeting hall was a room with flags of the PRC, North Korea, Vietnam, and Cuba. The Christians began to wave these flags and claim these nations for Christ. They wanted to evangelize them. They expressed gratitude for the Bibles that Christians from Europe and the US brought to them.

Pastor and his team handed out tracts in the Red Square. Soldiers readily received them. His team saw many conversions. A crippled was healed after 12 years of being lame. As he returned to HK, he wept and prayed, "O Lord, please let this happen in China too."

Many cults had proselytized the Russians. The cult leaders diligently prepared and supported their followers to learn Russian. They equipped scores of witnesses to convert people in the PRC too. Christians need to bring the Gospel to Russia and China.

I praised the Lord because three of my English class students were reading their Bibles. Nine out of eleven of my students believed in Jesus. Such joy!

Sherry's mother returned to the US on March 9. Before she departed, she visited the Vietnamese at Shek Kong camp. She was shocked at the deplorable conditions in which they lived. Families lived in Quonset huts on shelves stacked three high. The children lacked sufficient clothes. The camp was dirty. The stench of the outdoor toilets stuck to your clothes long after you left the camp. Rapes, fights, and murders were common. Surprisingly, the refugees said the camp was better than Vietnam. One refugee, who recently returned to Vietnam, reported that the customs official was ready to confiscate the Bible we gave him, but he begged for permission to keep it. He said, "Please take all my belongings, but don't take my Bible!" So, they took all his belongings and let him keep his Bible. Then, they sent him to work in the countryside.

The Lord provided a helper for Sherry. Her name was Mrs. Wan. She had three teenage sons. She was a Christian widow from our church. She cleaned for two hours three times per week. With her help, Sherry regained strength. Our fourth child was due to be born on May 25.

On April 17, I dreamed that the believers in Guangzhou were in trouble. The next day, I received news that one had been sent to the countryside for re-education. The Holy Spirit brought Scripture to mind while I was meditating on their situation. Acts 20:28-30 says, "Therefore take heed to yourselves and to all the flock, among which the Holy Spirit has made you overseers, to shepherd the church of God which He purchased with His own blood. For I know this, that after my departure savage wolves will come in among you, not sparing the flock. Also, from among yourselves men will rise, speaking perverse things, to draw away the disciples after themselves."

On Monday, I visited Guangzhou not knowing what might happen to me. Last week, a missionary was arrested. He was interrogated for four hours and then, released. The believers informed me that two of our group members had been sent to the countryside by their work units as punishment for their faith in God. Surprisingly, they both reported that they were doing well. One, a medical doctor, said that she enjoyed lengthy times of fellowship with the Lord. The other believer, Fang Na, reported that she was breathing better because she was far from the city's smog. She also made new friends.

A third believer reported that she resigned her high paying job due to her boss asking her to falsify company records. She refused to do it. She started serving God full-time by faith. She planned to distribute Gospel tracts on Sunday.

Someone told me that the pastor of the largest church in Guangzhou had been arrested. This was a false report. A meeting led by African university students continued despite threats of arrest. We spoke with Lydia. She was fine. In fact, she said her son-in-law was ready for me to preach to his factory workers.

The devil tried to quench the passion of these believers for Jesus but failed. Our Lord blessed them and made them to be blessings. His Spirit was strongly at work in them.

During the last five months of sickness and persecution, I confessed my short-comings and learned to rely on God's grace more. I spent more time with my Abba Father. I even went to special places where I could pray without interruption. During my times of communion with our Heavenly Father, I envisioned doors of opportunity opening. The Father showed me that there was a price to pay, a cost to count and a plan to make, but that He was with me. With God nothing is impossible!

On May 14, Sherry revived physically and spiritually. She led the children out to distribute Gospel tracts on two occasions while I was gone. People commented that she was like a new person. This meant so much to me because I love Sherry. Her love for me inspired me to go extra miles for Jesus.

Mercy was born on May 28 at Prince of Wales Hospital in Sha Tin. Sherry was seriously ill earlier in the year, but both Mercy and Sherry were healthy and happy after the birth. We named our dear baby Mercy because the Lord had been very merciful to us. We were happy and so were Mercy's siblings.

The authorities assigned Dr. Janet to do medical work in a village. They forced her to read political speeches. Fang Na was initially healthy, but her health took a severe turn for the worse. She entered a hospital in poor condition. Pastor Samuel Lamb was arrested on March 24. He was interrogated for several hours and then, released. They put constant pressure on him to submit his congregation to government control.

According to a Yunnan Province Christian worker, the PSB had launched an extensive re-education program for party cadres. The leaders highlighted the role the Church played in the downfall of communism in Eastern European. The campaign reportedly included a video lecture featuring a senior New China News Agency (NCNA) journalist. He reported, "The Church played an important role in the change. If China does not want such a scene to be repeated in its land, it must strangle the baby [of Christianity] while it is still in the manger." Isn't that what Herod tried to do during the toddler days of Jesus? He tried to kill Jesus before He grew up.

On May 1, Janet phoned us to say that she would be released from "political re-education camp" for 10 days. She asked if we could meet at the "fellowship place." On May 4, I was surprised to see Janet, AND seven other Chinese, three of which had never heard the Gospel before. They wanted to hear about Jesus. One of the newcomers professed faith in Christ.

It was a happy reunion. Those who knew me were amazed how much my Cantonese had improved. They asked me to return to Guangzhou on a weekly basis to teach them more about Jesus. They were determined to move forward with the Lord, to sing loudly, to pray beautifully and to testify boldly! Praise God!

The directors of RCC's Vietnamese Ministry asked me to direct the ministry once again. This time from June 15 – August 15. It was a privilege to serve the Lord this way. The "Vietnamese ministry" involved feeding several hundred hungry souls for God.

Annie Yun worked full-time and attended night school. She was weary. Sometimes she was so depressed that she could neither talk nor nod her head when we talked to her. On one occasion, when nothing seemed to help, I asked Grace, Glory and Andrew to talk with her. When they did, she started smiling and talking again. Sherry also spoke and prayed with her. She ate supper with us last Sunday and seemed to be better. She struggled with work, school, and a broken home. We prayed for her.

On June 15, I knocked on the door of Fang Na's old apartment building. She was back. She looked down from her balcony and exclaimed, "Ah Mak - oh Hallelujah!" She was free. She was healed. She kept saying, "Gamjeh Jyu" (Thank You Lord) as she explained how the Lord had been with her during her time of detention.

On June 22, I met with Janet and her father at Fang Na's apartment. Janet reported that soon she would be released from re-education camp two days per week. She brought her father with her so I could share the Gospel with him, which I did. He prayed afterwards. He also thanked the Lord for granting him a successful cataract surgery. Janet was full of joy. She shared with me revelations that the Lord gave her while detained.

On June 22, I took a $52 offering to Pastor Lamb. It was from a former member of his church who lived in the US. Lamb laughed as he told me how his government constantly urged him to submit his church to communist control. The government threatened his church member's wages via their work units. They spread lies about him saying that he made a young girl pregnant. Even so, his church grew. More than 1,100 people attended his services per week. He gave me a copy of a letter from the US Department of State. The letter stated that both Secretary of State Mr. James Baker and Assistant Secretary of State for Human Rights and Humanitarian Affairs, Mr. Richard Schifter, had spoken to their Chinese counterparts concerning freedom of religion in China. He appreciated their support. He suffered from hardening of arteries in his head. I prayed for him before I left.

Mercy shared the following written testimony with me about her salvation experience at Da Ma Zhan Church: "I remember the first time I went to Church. The topic of Pastor Samuel Lamb's sermon was "The Lord on the Cross." He preached that Jesus Christ bore insult, suffered hardship, and died

155

on the cross, just for our sin. When I heard this, my heart was deeply moved by His great love. I repented in tears and decided to accept a new life from Him. His love got rid of my self-abasement. His love gave me life and everything! Just as the hymn says: 'I was nothing until You found me. You have given life to me.' Yes, apart from Christ, I have no good thing."

The Lord moved on the heart of a Christian man to return $3,800 to his company through me. He had been allotted this money for business travelling expenses. During his trip, he saw an opportunity to defect. He and his wife were studying in a seminary to prepare for full-time ministry. He did not want the Chinese government to know he was alive, so he asked me to return the money. Everything went well. None of Guangzhou's numerous pickpockets got the money. The company did not detain me. The police did not seize me for questioning. They did not ask for my identity. When I refused to give them any information about their former employee, they let me go. I praised God for my brother's integrity and for the Lord's help to me.

Three former members of the Guangzhou fellowship have asked us to pray that God will move the US government to renew their visa permissions to stay in the US. Their visas were about to expire. One was a doctor. He shared the Gospel with his patients and hosted a Bible study in his home. He urged other overseas Chinese to attend church.

The Vietnamese ministry grew. There were over 55 missionaries working in three camps. The poor heard the good

156

news. Unbelievers believed in Christ. Prayers were answered. We were excited, but then, after one brief meeting with the head of the Social Services Department, our excitement dampened. He banned short-term volunteers from the camp due to the amount of paperwork each volunteer generated for his staff members. I responded to his news with a plea for reconsideration. I told him that we could not accomplish what was expected of us without the help of short-term volunteers. I also presented to him a policy sheet which volunteers were to sign. Volunteers were expected to comply with the expectations of the Social Services Department. This did not change his mind.

The Social Services Department allowed our long-term volunteers (six months or more) to keep serving. We had 32 missionaries qualified to serve. Thankfully, the new Social Services Department policy regarding volunteers was equally applied to all organizations.

The directors of the Vietnamese ministry returned to HK on August 20. While they were gone, the Lord blessed us with four new volunteers for the ministry. Two new financial supporters! Two leadership training meetings for the refugees were added to the weekly schedule. The trainings aimed to prepare them to lead Christian meetings back in Vietnam.

The entire Shek Kong Camp was to be closed within two months. Many refugees were relocated to camps that were closed to us. All refugees were to be evacuated before the end of 1994.

Churches in Vietnam were infiltrated by communist troublemakers who undermined the work of Christ among the people. Some of our missionaries planned to seek secular employment in Vietnam so that they could continue to disciple our camp's converts. Others planned to use HK as a base from which to launch short-term trips to Vietnam for the sake of the ministry among these people.

During June, a 17-year-old, Biu began to partner with me in spreading the Gospel in the PRC and in the refugee camp. He was on summer vacation from school. He taught me Cantonese. Biu and I prayed for a man in Shenzhen who had his second relapse of tuberculosis. Several days later, his son told us that he felt immediately better after we prayed for him and was healed thanks to Jesus. I thanked the Lord for Biu. Once, when a police officer asked him to open his bag of Bibles, he did not flinch. I told the men that Biu was carrying my bag for me. He let us go without checking the bag. Praise the Lord! Biu remained steadfast in his commitment to work alongside of me.

Last winter, I spoke with a man named David Cheng for two hours during an outreach event. He wanted me to pray for him but was not ready to profess Christ as his Lord and Savior. However, later, he came to church on his own. In July, he enrolled into RCMI's Bible College. He shared Scriptures with us when we met with him. Glory to God!

Mr. Bill Fisher lifted his hands in worship to God. He had the joy of the Lord. Last Sunday, he contributed $123 to RCMI.

Sherry and I first met Bill in 1987 when he was an Anglican school teacher. We met him while walking on the sidewalk. He invited us out to eat. A few months ago, I met him again while I was handing out Gospel tracts at a public venue. He started attending RCC after that encounter.

The third term for my evangelistic English classes began. 30 students enrolled. Shane Chan taught seven beginner level students. I taught 23 intermediate level students.

From July 26 – 30, Pastor Jeong Seok and his wife Misook Gho travelled with me to the far northern city of Harbin, China. Harbin is near the Russian border and above North Korea. The Gho's were originally from South Korea. They have lived in the US for 10 years. We met Jeong and Misook while we were students at Concordia in River Forest, Illinois. Jeong and Misook were my lunchtime prayer partners. God used them to encourage me to pray for the PRC and to consider serving there. Jeong was the pastor at "Our Shepherd Church" in Lombard, Illinois.

We carried Bibles, teaching books and six children's illustrated Bible story books into China. The x-ray machine at the airport detected our books, but the guard gave me a kind smile and passed me through. We were not followed.

The Gho's had Korean Chinese friends in Harbin who were communist party members. We stayed with them. The Gho's preached the Gospel to our hosts while the TV was featuring a program about the abilities and talents of the People's Liberation Army. During the second night of our stay, the father believed in

Christ. On the third night, he was baptized. I prayed for him to be healed of arteriosclerosis. The electrical-like presence of the Holy Spirit could be felt as I prayed.

There was no shower, bathroom sink nor laundry machine in their home. We washed ourselves by using bowls of water that had been hand carried into the home. I washed my clothes on a washboard while sitting on a six-inch stool. We sat on the floor while eating. I was the first American they had ever seen. The day we left Harbin, the family pleaded for us to come back again.

Pastor Dennis asked me to take Dr. Bob Weiner with me to China. Bob was the founder of Maranatha Ministries. He had travelled to 60 countries. Maranatha had branch ministries in 20 countries. We got Bibles through the border and delivered them safely to our contacts. We also visited Pastor Lamb and found that his health had improved. He had not been arrested since April. His church had over 1,200 attendees.

What amazed me about Bob was his sensitivity to the Holy Spirit. We were walking on the campus of Zhongshan University. Suddenly, he said, "Him!" "There!" He pointed to a man sitting on a bench. Bob told me to reach out to the man. The man stood up before I got to him and approached me. He asked me, "Do you have a Bible?" The Holy Spirit had led me to save one Chinese Bible just in case I met someone who needed one. I told the man, "Yes!" I gave him the Bible. He was grateful. He had been praying for one. Praise the Lord!

I took missionary Dave Snyder into the PRC. Dave served the Lord in Mexico for 10 years and in the Philippines for one year. He and his wife planned to return in the future. They felt called to do full-time service to the Lord in the PRC.

Three pastors from the US asked me to travel with them in the PRC. Their names were Pastor Jim Armstrong, Pastor James Bruce, and Evangelist Hobart Vann. We travelled together on September 15. I shared with them about the needs of the people.

At 3 am on September 9, an American pastor telephoned his wife. He was in Wuyang. She was in HK. The pastor had been holding a three-day conference with a 160-pastors when suddenly, he was told to leave immediately. 40 police officers with walkie talkies closed in on their location. The locals put the American pastor in a horse drawn cart and covered him up as though he was a corpse. They pulled him away swiftly. One Singaporean escaped while another was arrested. A Malaysian and a Chinese American were arrested. 120 of the 160 pastors were arrested. The American arrived in HK on September 11. The Singaporean who escaped arrived in HK on September 15. The other Singaporean and Malaysian ministers were held for a week. They were bound with ropes and interrogated. The Chinese American was detained until September 25. The 120 local pastors remained in detention.

A Wuyang Christian reported that the PSB entered the homes of believers to confiscate their valuables and to fine them. Neighbors raided their homes because they knew that the government would neither protect nor defend them. One sister was beaten severely. Many were handcuffed and tied up. Their money, computers, cameras, and their Bibles were confiscated. An offering of $1,500 from Christians in Shandong to those in Wuyang was confiscated.

Christians had been meeting for years in this location where the arrests took place. They had never experienced trouble before. There was no government approved church in this part of Henan for Christians to meet at. The meeting had been organized by local Christians.

We continued to take Bibles into the PRC. Three American pastors helped me move about 200 pounds of Bibles. They met with my Guangzhou contacts, shared Scripture with them and prayed for them. Hobart Vann also shared at a meeting that I arranged for him in HK. One man believed in Jesus after hearing him preach the Gospel.

Huang C. Ming of Christian Born Anew Fellowship (CBAF) offered to pay my airfare, food, and accommodation expenses for a trip to Taiwan. I arrived in Taipei at 11 pm on October 3. Huang arranged for me to speak at a Baptist Church, Ming-Che Church, a Junior High School, a family meeting, an evening house meeting, a bankers' fellowship, the Formosa Plastic Corporation, a military prison, another Baptist Church and to do daily devotions with the staff members of Born Anew Fellowship. Taiwan was 2.5% Christian. Many people worshipped idols. Huang urged me to preach the cross and to call people to obey the Lord.

During October, 17 Taiwanese souls believed in Christ. Seven of these new believers were prisoners. I had the privilege to pray for 80 prisoners who wanted the Lord to heal them. An abandoned mother of three children professed faith in Christ. A second abandoned mother shared with me how her house burned down, and after that, she was robbed. The Lord healed a small girl who had a rash for months. The rash disappeared! Glory to God!

One Baptist Church had me preach on two Sundays. The ministry there lasted from morning until evening. I also did a Wednesday evening meeting for them. Their pastor had just died from cancer two weeks prior to my arrival. They found it difficult to understand why God would allow such a godly and faithful man die of cancer. The Lord provided me appropriate Scriptures to share with them. The Word of God lifted their countenances including that of the pastor's widow. They especially wanted teaching on the Holy Spirit and His gifts. Two of the members received the gift of speaking in tongues. The people invited me to their homes and out to eat three times while I was there. One member drove me around in his Mercedes-Benz and took me out to eat at the Grand Hotel. This was because his brother had given his life to Jesus after I shared the Gospel with him. Alleluia!

One deacon named Stanley was on fire for God. He prayed and read his Bible throughout the day. He witnessed for Christ to those around him. He gave generously to the church. His job previously required him to travel abroad often. He no longer travelled abroad due to kidney malfunction. His wife, Sherry, did the travelling for him. He imported machinery from abroad.

The largest corporation in Taiwan was the Formosa Plastic Corporation. The Lord opened the door for me to share with a group of the white-collar workers at this corporation. I shared with the workers from Ezekiel about not whitewashing our shattered lives. I urged them to come to God for healing. One man asked Christ to save him. Four others asked for prayer.

Seven students at a junior high school believed in Christ after I shared the Gospel with them. I also had the privilege to share testimonies about the Christians in the PRC at a Banker's Christian Fellowship meeting. One evening, after supper, I met a 27-year-old lady named Tesserina (a Buddhist name). She was a devout Buddhist. Her father had just died. I shared Scripture with her for nearly two hours. She believed in Christ. She was visibly uplifted by and grateful for Jesus. Glory to God!

I had the privilege to lead devotions at the beginning of five different workdays for the staff members of CBAF. They asked me Bible questions. CBAF primarily served prisoners but received invitations to speak in many locations. They gave me a $300 honorarium. I used the money for trips to Guangzhou.

Grace, Glory and Andrew sang Scripture songs to several of our Wednesday evening English students. I was grateful that God sent young people to visit Sherry and the children while I was in Taiwan. They helped Sherry to take the children to a nearby park to play. Annie Yun brought food and cooked for them. They experienced peace while I was gone. Praise God!

Concerning the 120 pastors in Wuyang that were arrested during September, 14 of these pastors were released. The price for the remaining pastors to be released was $127.27 per pastor. RCMI sent $13,003.90 to cover this cost, plus extra money for the pastors to take with them. The bail was paid for the pastors little by little so as not to arouse suspicion about the money's origins.

Sherry ministered to the Chinese directly and indirectly. Indirectly, she raised our four children to be missionaries. She helped Grace and Glory to memorize Scriptures and Bible-oriented songs. They prayed for the people that we served. She practiced hospitality. One Guangzhou disciple told us that it was our children whom God used to draw her to us. Others have said the same. Showing hospitality was how Sherry ministered to others while caring for our children.

Lydia, Mr. Wu, and Persis came to HK this month. Mr. Wu paid their way. Mainlanders can come to HK for $150 for seven days, but then, must leave again. Lydia and Persis came to our home for lunch. It was their first time to see baby Mercy. They had not seen Sherry and the children since December 1991. It was a happy reunion. Persis was expecting her first baby and Lydia's first grandchild.

Lydia, Persis, and Mr. Wu joined our Sunday service at RCC. Lydia shared a 15-minute salvation testimony. She described the people of the PRC as feeling hopeless. They lacked faith in Marxism. They believed in themselves and in making money. Many wanted to leave China.

During their visit, Mr. Wu asked us to come and share the Gospel in the shoe factory. He wanted us to come during the Chinese New Year holiday. This open door was an answer to the prayers of many.

Daughin was a young man in his 20's when he began to travel with me to Guangzhou each week. We led Christ-centered meetings at Zhongshan University. We had seven disciples. One of them cried as we prayed for her. We gave out 300 Gospel tracts to homeless people and told them about Jesus. We preached in Cantonese. Daughin led a lady at Zhongshan University named Mary to Jesus.

During December, our entire family did ministry. Sherry, Grace, Glory and Andrew sang for the Christmas Eve service at RCC. Grace, Glory and Andrew also sang before 500 students at a Lutheran Primary School. They sang a song entitled, "It's Amazing What Praising Can Do." After singing and picture taking, they enjoyed playing with the students. The school gave our children Christmas gifts.

Christmas Eve was special because two souls professed faith in Christ. I had the opportunity to follow up with another soul who had recently believed. One of the converts was a Wednesday evening English student from Shane's class. The other two, I encountered on the corner of Argyle Street and Nathan Road in Mongkok. Every year, we did an outreach on

Christmas Eve at this corner. About 80 of our members did witnessing, singing, and testifying from 10:30 pm until 1:30 am. Many people believed in Jesus. Our outreach team included people from HK, Singapore, Taiwan, Japan, South Korea, Nepal, England, Germany, Ireland, and the US.

On New Year's Eve, I wrote down goals for the New Year. They were to lead young people to evangelize in HK; to lead HK people to evangelize in Guangzhou; to keep teaching English classes for witnessing purposes; disciple whomsoever was willing to serve Jesus; to offer godly counsel to whoever came to us; and to pray at church for one hour per day. Sherry's goal was to keep promoting Biblical family values.

~ Chapter 10 ~
Called by the Gospel (1993)

February 22 – 23, the Lord blessed our family and others to bring the Gospel to 1,200 factory workers. We distributed a case of Gospel literature to them. We invited them to a meeting inside a large empty room within the compound. About 100 employees joined the meeting. Sherry, Glory and Andrew sang songs in Chinese. Lemuel, Daughin, Susan, Wen Ying, Lydia, and I shared testimonies. Evangelist Harley Fiddler preached.

Towards the end of Harley's message, a fight started outside the room in which we were meeting. Nearly everyone left the room to watch the fight. When Harley gave the invitation to believe in Christ, about 20 workers raised their hands indicating that they wanted to believe in Jesus.

Harley had shared with me prior to the meeting that he had a vision of people being healed by God's power. So, before he closed the meeting, I announced that when Jesus sent His disciples out to preach the Good News, He also told them to heal the sick. Then, I asked, "Does anyone need healing?" One man came forward. Harley, Susan, and I prayed for him, and he was healed immediately. Then, others came forward for healing. Soon, the people outside the room came rushing back in. We were surrounded by a sea of people in fulfillment of Harley's vision. A woman with a lump on her foot was healed. The lump disappeared. The healings continued from 9:30 pm – 11:30 pm.

On top of the healings, more than 100 workers professed faith in Christ for the first time. Praise the Lord! It was a miracle! Jesus did the work through His Word and Spirit. We were His vessels.

The next day, an influential professor of history, literature and culture professed faith in Christ. This same professor had previously laughed and joked about Jesus. Harley spoke to him. Daughin interpreted. The Holy Spirit converted the man's soul.

We visited Lily and her mother. Lily was pregnant. It should have been a happy moment, but the father wanted her to abort the baby. He rejected his responsibility.

Lily was concerned that the government would force her to abort the baby. Her mother earned $17 per month. They lived in a privately-owned apartment. The landlord knew of Lily's pregnancy. She used this knowledge to demand $170 per month rent from her mother. This was an unreasonable amount! If she did not pay it, the landlord would evict her. We urged Lily to trust God and to save her baby. We placed them before God by prayer.

On February 14, Lemuel, Susan, Daughin and I led a hotel worker to faith in Christ. This worker had six people in her home who wanted to study the Bible. Praise God!

On March 28, I wrote of answered prayers. Lily was grateful that we urged her to preserve her unborn child's life. Pastor Dennis visited Lily and urged her to believe God for a husband and not to fix her mind on adopting this baby to someone outside of China. Daughin and Bernie visited Lily's mother and found her happy and jumping for joy to see them.

A house meeting was underway in the Dong Shan District now that we had a leader for that group. One Christian there wanted to be baptized. A Sister Mai informed us of a group Christians that was seeking a pastor. We welcomed them in.

Kok Fai and Syut Hong helped us. The Guangzhou ministry provided an excellent opportunity for them to practice what they learned at church. They were excited to join us. The cost of the trips to Guangzhou averaged $120 per week. We were still covering the traveling expenses for those who joined us.

Last December, our monthly income trended-upward so I started bringing more volunteers with me. We received $2,562.22 during December 1992. I had no pre-indicator that our income would dip during the first quarter while ministry expenses would increase. I taught English to earn an extra $75 per month.

It was April 13. The post office was closed for four days in honor of Easter. We had less than $10 and only two days-worth of food. Thanks to God we better understood the sufferings of Christ on the cross through this experience. We cried as we watched a video of a passion play performed by the members of Full Faith Church of Love West in Kansas City. In the video, Jesus delivered people from bondages. He suffered hatred and rejection while dying for our sins. We cried as we watched Jesus welcomed into heaven as angels sang, "We shall behold Him, and be changed in a moment." Our sacrifices were so that lost souls would hear the Gospel and be ready for Christ's return.

On Saturday, I checked the mailbox at church. We seldom received mail in this box. There was a letter in our box with a check for $100 enclosed. Then, on Sunday, we received $389.62 in offerings from local believers who did not know the depths of our need. $194.81 was designated for us personally and $194.81 was designated for the ministry to Guangzhou. This was a type of resurrection experience for us. The enemy has told us that our mission was over, but God redeemed and resurrected it.

On April 6, accommodations were offered to us for our weekly trips to Guangzhou. This FREE apartment saved us $1,520 per month. Our ministry team consisted of seven members. Instead of having one large meeting each week, we divided into three ministry teams and held three smaller meetings simultaneously. The free apartment and the smaller meeting strategy breathed new life into the Guangzhou ministry.

A motorcyclist and a taxi driver believed in Christ after Daughin invited them to our meeting. A week later, we found them still shining. The taxi driver wanted to be baptized. He transported us free of charge on numerous occasions.

Towards the end of April, RCC unanimously approved a monthly stipend of $1,028 to support our discipleship ministry. Praise God for answered prayer! Our season of poverty passed. The result of our seed falling and dying – preaching the Gospel despite numerous hardships – was a 180 saved souls.

Jesus Christ died on the cross for me an unworthy sinner. I loved Jesus with my whole being. Last Sunday, I spoke in both services on the life of Stephen the martyr. He was dedicated to serving people and the church. I wanted to emulate him.

Recently, two Christians who helped a missionary were arrested by PSB agents. The PSB dressed like common people, even like beggars. It was hard to detect them. God's grace helped us to evade them. The PRC government suspected Americans of fomenting "Peaceful Revolution" among their people. To them, the freedom of religion message was a ploy to incite a coup.

Sherry continued to help children memorize Scripture. 20 Vietnamese memorized Psalm 23, John 3:16-17, John 1:12 and John 14:12. Sherry arranged someone to translate the verses and badges into Vietnamese. Three missionary children memorized and received badges. Grace and Glory earned three badges each. Badges were translated into Tagalog for Filipinas. We purchased badge parts, colored them, and assembled them ourselves.

During June, Yat Ming and Wai Ha received Christ after I shared the Gospel with them. A taxi driver received Christ after my co-workers Daughin and Neil shared the Gospel with them. We preached the Gospel on trains, in parks and in the homes. Yat Ming and Wai Ha joined our Guangzhou Fellowship group.

This month, RCC asked me to be "Keui Jeung" (Zone Leader or Overseer) in the Student Fellowship. I was to mobilize the students to serve for the Lord. I hoped to plant discipleship meetings in each of Guangzhou's six districts. Guangzhou's six districts were: Yuht Sau (Beyond Excellence), Dùng Sàan (East Mountain), Hói Jyù (Pearl Sea), Baahk Wàhn (White Cloud), Tìn

Hòh (Sky River) and Li Wan (Li Bay). The meetings would be led by pairs of missionaries. One would preach, the other would lead the singing, share a testimony, and pray for the people.

I managed three home group meetings per week in Guangzhou. I bought train tickets for the team members. We boarded a train in Shenzhen shortly after 10 am. We arrived in Guangzhou by early afternoon. During the afternoons, we did visitations. The home group meetings took place between 5:30-7:30 pm. We boarded an 8:15 pm train back to HK and reached the border by 11 pm. The train tickets were $14.30 for each person with a HK-ID card or $19.50 otherwise. Each ministry pair received $14 to hire taxis.

On June 16, I wrote a letter to Sherry's parents, "The children loved the letters from you. They carried the letters around for a while. They are blessed to have grandparents who care for them so much. Sadly, I am at the hospital with Glory as I write this letter. Glory has gastroenteritis with fever. Despite her pain, she is sitting next to me and pretending that she is talking on the phone with Mandy Knosp and Mommy." Glory was released from the hospital the next day. By then, she was able to eat a large lunch without experiencing stomach pain. Her fever was gone.

Steve Robinson married a Vietnamese woman named Mai from the refugee camp. He prayed for many years to meet the right woman. He asked us to pray as well. God answered his prayer and ours beyond what we could have asked or imagined. He and Mai were very happily married.

On July 2, I wrote a letter to Sherry's parents, "I am playing with the children as I write you. Glory likes the Sandi Patti Christmas tape that you sent us. We enjoyed listening to it even as we played blocks together. I built the children a telephone with string for a wire, as well as an oven large enough to cook their plastic food in, and a pretend vacuum cleaner. It was fun. Later, while outdoors, we practiced throwing a tennis ball-sized hard fruit through a hole in a dead tree. God is good!"

Recently, the pastor of Abundant Life Church in St. Louis read a letter that I wrote to his whole congregation. It really touched him. He read it many times and wept as he did. He used my letter as a rallying point to urge his church to keep supporting us, to keep praying for us and to encourage others to do missionary service. An article was also written about us in a brochure that was distributed at a mission conference that took place at Life Christian Center. Praise God!

I joined the youth group at RRC to improve my ability to understand and speak Cantonese. I befriended the Christian brothers so that the Lord could speak into their lives through me. I also prayed for them. Last week, three of the brothers joined me in ministry to Guangzhou.

Salvations during June included a man from India. He renounced Hinduism and idolatry. He started attending church. A man in Guangzhou also believed in Christ after I shared the Gospel with him for about an hour.

As a teenager, I wrote a poem entitled, "Some Day One Day." Later, I composed a novel entitled, "Darkness will Fall on the City." The novel told the story of a futuristic Christian crusader who wore armor to protect himself against evil. There were no worship services in his city because churches were closed. His society was wicked. The crusader had two faithful disciples. The goal of both the poem and the unpublished novel was to inspire me to act on God's Word. Don't procrastinate. James 4:17 says, "If anyone, then, knows the good they ought to do and doesn't do it, it is sin for them." The Lord urged me via Zechariah 4:10 not to despise the day of small things." We must start small and keep building.

One day, while walking and praying through a portion of Guangzhou, I saw two cathedrals that were being used for commercial purposes. After I saw these closed churches, I remembered the story that I wrote as a teen. Here I was in Guangzhou planting churches where a government had closed them. There were only a couple of churches in this city of more than six million people. The population of Guangzhou was greater than the population of more than sixty countries of our world. The Lord had me on a crusade. These people needed the Lord.

A key Bible verse that I claimed for Guangzhou was Daniel 2:44, "The God of heaven will set up a kingdom that will never be destroyed, nor will it be left to another people. It will crush all those kingdoms and bring them to an end, but it will itself endure forever." I rejected the lie of "Some-Day-One-Day"

175

procrastination. I rejected the lie of darkness being greater than light. I believed in a victorious Lord! A glorious Gospel! Captives set free by the power of God!

On August 21, I wrote a letter to Sherry's parents, "Couriers move about 7,000 Bibles over the border per month. I drive the church's van and the box truck to help out. I use the van to transport short-term missionaries from the airport to missionary housing. I use the box truck to transport Bibles from one warehouse to another. Last night, I moved 1,265 pounds of Bibles. The truck sits six-passengers, so Sherry and the children sometimes accompany me during these labors of love.

There have been over 20 salvations in Guangzhou since the last letter. Believers from RCC's student fellowship are yielding good fruit. 10 students joined my ministry team this week. We split into four teams and ministered in four districts at the same time. Glory to God!

On September 6, I wrote, "Last week, I sat in The Great Hall of the People on the edge of Tiananmen Square. I was a part of a trade delegation. 12 nations were represented. All my expenses were paid. Right smack dab inside the PRC's supreme court, a Chinese man believed in Jesus Christ through the witness of a Chinese-speaking American pastor! There were high government officials present. Amazing!!!

I had assisted 175 foreign businessmen to deliver 13,000 of 15,000 Bibles to the PRC. 1,792 Bibles were confiscated after one of our delegates was stopped. This stop, led to those behind him in line being stopped and checked for Bibles. I stayed behind with those who were stopped. Amazingly, the border guards never asked to see my passport. We praised God for 88% success. After the meeting in the Great Hall, we went to parks and tourist sites and preached the Gospel. And estimated 40 people professed faith in Christ. One taxi driver said that he had heard the Name of Jesus 20 years prior to our arrival. He had been waiting all these years for someone to tell him more. He professed faith in Christ. Others told us that they had never heard the Gospel before. This happened between August 30 – September 2.

A couple from Guangzhou came to Beijing to join up with us. Joseph was not a Christian when he arrived in Beijing, but he professed faith in Christ on the night he arrived. Joseph and Mary helped us handout Gospel tracts. I taught them Bible doctrines while we rode together on the tour bus.

A few months ago, three of our co-workers were detained briefly by the PSB while handing out tracts near the Joseph's home. Mary saw the co-workers being escorted away. In less than an hour, the co-workers were free, and she welcomed them into her home. She asked us to keep teaching the Bible in her home.

We visited Lily and her mother during our last trip. Lily's mother, Feng Na, had a reoccurring growth on her foot which needed to be removed by surgery. Lydia invited Lily to stay in her home until she found a new place. We gave Lily $65 to find an apartment. We committed to help her in this way for three months. One of my local contacts supplied the name of an elderly person to watch Lily's baby while she worked. The Guangzhou Christians made sacrifices so that baby "Grace" could live.

Young people from RCC helped me to serve special needs teenagers at the Zhiling school. They led them to sing Christian songs. Among the HK young people who joined my weekly trips to Guangzhou were Biu, Wai Kit and Kok Fai. Many special needs teens prayed to Jesus. We also witnessed to the teachers and volunteers. Zhiling served as a training field for young Christians to develop their ministry skills. We were blessed with 22 converts to Christ. One convert was a soldier. Another a policeman!

The Lord answered another prayer. He provided a Christian school for Grace and Glory to attend. Praise the Lord!

Two sisters in Guangzhou helped us to rent an apartment for $118 per month. The apartment had four bedrooms. Lily and her baby stayed in the largest room. My HK team members stayed in the other two rooms one night per week. The men's bedroom was a separate apartment from the other apartment. Neighbors did not see our team members enter the same door that Lily and her mother entered. We invested 100's to rent this apartment, move Lily and her mother's there and to furnish it. We also partially supported Lily and her baby. Amazingly, the expenses were still less costly then renting rooms at a hotel for my team of six each week. We called this apartment, "The House of Refuge." Our prayer for Lily and her daughter Grace was that the Lord would provide them a new husband and father to take care of them [which the Lord did later].

Since our last newsletter, 16 more souls were added to God's kingdom. On October 3, another taxi driver professed faith in Christ. A sister who witnessed his conversion and his in-filling by the Holy Spirit, asked us to pray for her to receive the baptism of the Holy Spirit.

Matt Bell arrived on September 17. He is from Life Christian Center in St. Louis. He was a big help to the China Bible ministry. He helped me to move Lily's things from their old apartment to the new one. He helped me to reach out to young people at RCC. An RN sister from Life Christian Center also applied to come and work at RCC.

Grace and Glory liked their new school in the village. Their teacher, Rheba Carter, and her husband Glen started this school. They supported my work into Guangzhou generously. We paid $100 per month for Grace and Glory to attend their school. Our home served as a lunchroom for the school's seven students.

On October 16, the HK newspaper reported that two Christian meetings in Guangzhou were raided by plain clothed PSB officers. Everyone's identification was checked. The leaders were taken in for questioning but released after several hours. All Bibles, hymnals and address books were taken from the members. These Christians started branch churches of the Da Ma Zhan Church. Pastor Lamb told me that officials held a meeting in Guangzhou's Dong Shan District. At that meeting, they decided that he must be forced to register his church with the government or be shut down. The government plan was to demolish the entire block where his church was located. Pastor Lamb said that if he registered his church, he would no longer be able to teach or baptize people younger than 18, and his teaching would have had to adhere to Marxist doctrine.

There were 14 salvations in Guangzhou during November. 15 converts were baptized in water. Praise the Lord!

While worshiping God at a meeting in Panyu, a woman fell on the floor and began jerking around uncontrollably. She was screaming and crying. This happened right in front of me. The Spirit led me to command the evil spirit to depart from her in the Name of Jesus. Afterwards, she jumped up and began praising God. She went around the room and thanked everyone. Then, she testified how the evil spirit had kept her in a closet for a week at a time. She couldn't get out of the closet until it let her out. She repeated the words of a song that we had sung, saying, "Because He lives, I can face tomorrow, because He lives, all fear is gone."

On November 1, I wrote in my prayer diary, "Isaiah 58:6-17." This passage was about breaking the yoke of oppression. I prayed that Scripture back to God on many mornings. On November 26, when this woman was set free, I witnessed an answer to my Isaiah 58:6-17 prayer right before my eyes.

Another woman was a relatively new Christian. She had not repented of her former sins. As she repented of worshiping two idols, she became ice-cold all over. She also experienced pains in her shoulders and legs. When she renounced her former life of greed, she became short of breath. But after this time of repentance, she felt healthy and full of joy. A week later, she told us that since that day, she had experienced greater joy and peace in her life. She was worshiping God more than ever before.

Twice in November, teams of 20 Americans joined me in ministry to Guangzhou. The Celebrant Singers was one of the groups. The two music teams sang at the Zhiling School.

The Lord supplied sufficient finances to care for Lily and her baby. Baby Grace had no official birth certificate or identity card, but God knew her name. A HK sister named Karena Or stayed with Lily to help her. She discipled Lily. She prayed with Lily daily. On December 7, there was a robbery in the apartment above Lily's, but Lily and her baby were left untouched.

Lily and her mother reached out to people. They briefly housed a homeless lady from Beijing whose wallet and identity card had been stolen. The next day, Lily took her to the police station and helped her get new identification documents. Other Guangzhou Christians helped the lady out with money.

We praised God for the couple who let us use their home for a Bible teaching location. We praised God for the two taxi drivers who professed faith in Jesus. They provided us free rides each week. We praised God for Zhiling School.

Our son Andrew was the ring bearer in three weddings in two month's-time. We were blessed to see him walk down the wedding aisle with a Chinese flower girl. We praised God for the inclusive love that we experienced from the Chinese Christians.

~ Chapter 11 ~
Called by the Gospel (1994)

On January 20, I wrote, "Can a modern-day Christian love the Lord so much so that he or she is willing to risk losing everything for Him? Back in January of 1989, I assumed that I would never cower from going forward with Christ's work in Guangzhou. But then, my university authority figures began to visit my family and make subtle threats against us. Then, I heard of an American teacher whose daughter was murdered. Fear for what the authorities might do to Sherry or one of my children got the best of me. I left the PRC. That happened five years ago. During 41 of the last 60 months, I have constantly been in and out of the PRC doing the same work in the same places as before. What has made the difference? The difference was that my family was out of harm's way.

More than 20 people were joining me on weekly trips to Guangzhou. 40 HK young signed up to join me on a ministry trip in April. I needed to locate more teaching locations for them.

Recently, the PSB visited Lily's mother. They asked her where Lily was. The officer knew that they had been associating with foreigners.

Sherry longed to take our children to see our parents. It had been 41 months since our last visit. Now, we had a fourth child. In April, Grace and Glory had a month-long break from school due to their teachers being in the States. The cost for airfare for Sherry and children to fly roundtrip to the States was over $2,500. Our bank account consisted of faith in God to provide. Praise the Lord for His tender mercies. He gave us the victory through our Lord Jesus Christ. Jesus was the small stone spoke of in Daniel 2:44 destined to increase in size and consume the whole world. We trusted in Him for greater things!

On Monday, February 7, Chinese Premier Li Peng appeared on a nationwide telecast to the people of the PRC. He told the nation to avoid contact with foreigners who preach religion and distribute religious literature. He promised to punish offenders. He said that foreigners caught in these acts would be punished and expelled.

On February 10, at three am, three Americans, two Kong Kongese, an Indonesian couple and seven Chinese nationals, were arrested by the PSB in Henan. The foreigners were held five days. During that time, no one could contact their embassies. They were treated roughly. One was beaten. The police stole $13,000 cash from them. They stole their electronic devices. Thankfully, Daughin hid $1,000 in his shoe. They needed this money to return to HK. The police intentionally expelled them with "no" resources. The Chinese nationals remained in prison. Some were beaten severely.

Before this group returned to HK, the news media got wind of this story. TV, radio, and newspaper reporters were waiting to interview them. HK news outlets were abuzz with this story. One of the American pastors was requested by Congress, the Senate, the Trade Commission and the Security Council to give an account of what happened. After this, the Parliament in London asked him to share his testimony as well.

The American pastor had pictures and eyewitness accounts to verify the arrest of the Christians. These Christians were hardworking citizens. They did not protest when arrested. The police plundered their belongings.

The PSB contacted two people in our fellowship. On February 21, as I was standing at the customs booth in the PRC, four soldiers and three plain clothes men came and stood in front of me. One of them aimed a video camera at me during the whole time that my passport was being checked. As soon as my passport was inspected, I walked off. I never looked back. That night, we had an excellent meeting. One businessman believed in the Christ for the first time. The people in Guangzhou knew what happened in Henan, but still wanted to meet with us.

In January, Pastor Dennis purchased a new laptop. The Lord led him to give me his old one which was in new condition. He allowed me to use a printer at RCC. I greatly appreciated these gifts. It was time consuming to type my letters on a typewriter.

One week, I prayed to Jesus for a taxi driver to recover his confiscated driver's license before our next meeting. The next week, he had it. Praise God! Before this prayer of faith, he had been trying unsuccessfully for two months to get it back.

A homeless boy whose mother was in the hospital with epilepsy showed up at our meeting. He testified that one night while he slept on the street, someone reached down and shook him. When he woke up, he saw Jesus standing in white clothing. The Lord's face was aglow. This 16-year-old professed faith in Christ. His mother owed $2,325 to the hospital. He had raised $232.50 towards the bill. He was from Henan. Sister Wong and her family invited him to stay with them. After we got to know him better, he told us that his family attended Pastor Dennis's meetings in Henan. His family members wanted him to join Pastor's meetings, but he refused. He came to Guangzhou to make money not find Jesus. It amazed me that he ran from Pastor Dennis's preaching only to hear preaching via one of his co-workers. We helped him when nobody else would. One Christian brother gave him $130. That was like 11 months of wages for Henan people. He got a job and worked towards paying off the hospital bill. Before he joined our fellowship, he had dug through trash daily to find things to sell.

On March 14, one of my team members began to distribute Gospel tracts on a train. Almost immediately, three PSB agents converged on us. Karena witnessed to two of them. An Aussie named Ralph witnessed to the third one. The first one prayed to Jesus for salvation. Afterwards, he remarked, "I cannot express with words how I just felt. It was wonderful. Just like only Jesus and I were in the train and on-one else." His name card had, "The People's Republic of China, Public Security Bureau Office" printed on it. The second policeman also believed in Christ, but the third one declined. They let us go free. Normally,

PSB agents arrested foreigners who distributed Gospel literature and proselytize. The Lord was gracious to us and to them.

Ka Fai and Daughin continued to do Guangzhou ministry with me despite their arrest experience in Henan. Karena told me that she would rather go to hell than to see someone else go there. This was the heart Jesus, Paul and Moses had for souls (See Acts 2:27-31, 1 Peter 3:19, Romans 9:3, Exodus 32:31-33). When someone has such depth of love for souls, who can stop them from witnessing for Jesus? It was a privilege to coordinate this team. Our meetings ended at 10 pm, but most of my teammates wanted to keep speaking and praying for people until 11 pm.

During one meeting, we had Dr. Ralph W. Neighbour as our guest along with two other pastors. He was an author and teacher. He taught church multiplication methods. We had pastors from Singapore, Dallas, Pittsburgh, and Washington DC join our meetings. Each pastor was overjoyed to see what God was doing. They made remarks about the tremendous level of love, joy, and peace among the Chinese believers.

Lily's baby was nine months old. They were both doing well. The Lord continued to supply us the finances to support them at the rate of $200 per month.

In January, we ran into soldiers with guns nearby to Lily's apartment. As a result, we returned to renting cheap hotel rooms for our ministry team. The Lord provided the finances.

Sherry and the children were scheduled to arrive in the US on March 29 for a visit with her parents. God answered our prayers for finances for this trip. The Lord gave them safe travels and refreshing rest amidst her parents and siblings.

I enjoyed a meal with James Robison's International Director and with his camera man. They were on assignment to find out about orphanage work in the PRC. Pastor Dennis, Kathy and Sharon were there also. Pastor Dennis and Sharon have been translating the book, "Visions Beyond the Veil." This book was about the orphanage work that was done in China by the parents of Roland and Heidi Baker.

16 people were baptized on March 28. Two converted taxi drivers asked to be included in the baptism service. We rode in four taxis to reach the baptismal place. Two of the drivers were believers, but two were not. The believers shared about Jesus with the taxi drivers on the way to the lake. A minor miracle helped the men to believe in Jesus. One of the unbelieving taxi drivers locked his keys in the car. We were far from help. The believers prayed in the Name of Jesus for a miracle. Suddenly, the doors unlocked. After that, both gladly confessed faith in Christ and were baptized. Glory to God!

On April 4, we rented a room that could hold a large audience. There were about 50 Chinese in attendance. 15 of RCC's young people joined me on this trip. Happy led worship. Others did special songs, played musical instruments, did skits, and shared testimonies. Ka Fai preached the Gospel. One of three newcomers believed in Jesus. Many wanted to be prayed for. This meeting was held between a rock and a hard place. It was situated

187

between the district PSB headquarters and another building where I was briefly confronted by the PSB during 1988. This was the place the Lord had led me to rent. A HK teen gave $130 to defray the cost of this trip. All went well!

Three people believed in Christ during our April 11 trip. One of the new believers was a lady taxi driver. Her father had cancer. She asked us to pray for him.

Mary translated my message, "How to Change the World" into Chinese. Another student typed and printed it out. It was distributed to the believers. They liked the part about dying to self and living for Christ. Glory to God!

Two very special men went with me to Guangzhou. One was a pastor from Peru. He ran an orphanage, an ACE school, a Bible school, as well as a radio station and TV broadcast.

The Maoist Shining Path Terrorists made numerous life threats against him. Some of his co-workers were gunned down by communist guerillas. The communists tried to force the children of their victims to deny the Lord. When a child did not deny Christ, the communists would dismember one child and cook him, and make the other children eat the cooked child. Then, they would ask the next child if he was a Christian. Thousands have died martyrs' deaths. Revival broke out. He had more than 1,500 members in his church. He, his wife and two children moved forward by the grace of God. He has met with President Clinton. He has flown to the US and to Japan with the president of Peru. The other man who went with us was an Argentinean businessman. He was one of the 20 top wealthiest men in Peru. Their message to the people in Guangzhou was to keep praying, preaching, and standing with Jesus. They closed with, "Never Give Up!" Three people believed in Christ.

Pastor Dennis referred four Russians to me. They said, "Communism is a dead spirit in the former USSR. There is total freedom now." They can evangelize via TV, newspaper and in public places. Their church in Abakan, Siberia, had 1,500 members. Their sanctuary held 5,000 people. Their church began five years ago. New members were added on a weekly basis. They had 700 students in their Bible school. The pastor said that many had turned to Jesus. These four Russians helped me to distribute Gospel tracts in HK.

On April 25, a policewoman joined our Guangzhou meeting. Mary asked me in front of everyone, including the officer, "Are you not afraid she will arrest us?" I replied, "No, Jesus also loves the police. They protect us and face a lot of danger on our behalf. Besides, I believe Jesus will arrest her and she will believe in Him." She did not believe in Jesus that evening, but she did stay two hours after the meeting. She asked many questions about Jesus and the Bible. She warmly shook our hands and thanked us. During this meeting, I boldly declared that the Lord would build His church despite opposition.

Sherry and children arrived safely back from their month-long trip to the US. They visited with her parents, siblings, and relatives. She also visited my parents. It was difficult for Sherry's parents to let her, and the children return to HK, but they did.

Sherry and the children were happy to be back. Andrew and I hung a birdhouse outside that he got from his grandparents. On April 28, Grace, Glory, and their friend Mandy sang songs, recited Scriptures, and did a skit for nine Christians who gathered in our home. I derived much happiness from my family.

Part of our ministry involved duplicating Star Family videos. Their videos helped children to memorize Scriptures. The shows taught Scripture via songs, puppet shows, and little skits.

On May 16, six Singaporean Christians joined Lemuel and me to Guangzhou. 10 souls were birthed into Christ's kingdom. Four of the converts were teachers at Zhiling school. One was a student at the school. Five more believed in Jesus at the Guangzhou Fellowship Meeting.

On May 23, a New Zealander and Swiss sister joined Lemuel and me to the meeting. Although there were no new believers, the Gospel was shared with many for the first time, and they listened intently. As I shared about faith in God, one of the fellowship members began to cringe in pain with terrible stomach pain. He ate something that had spoiled. He was bent over in pain and his face was contorted. Everyone watched him and no longer listened to me. I prayed within my heart, "Lord, please show me what to do." Immediately He answered. I told the people, "When Jesus sent out His disciples, He gave them authority to cast out demons and heal the sick. When Jesus sends you out to preach,

He gives you authority. So now, we are going to pray for this brother, and the Lord's going to heal him." We prayed, and he was instantly healed. Afterwards, he sang a song, shed a few tears, and told us, "We should all preach the Gospel. And if we have two coats, we should share with him who has none." Praise the Lord for His grace. Our visitors said that they had sensed God's anointing upon this meeting. Glory to Jesus!

On May 2, a police lady, and her boyfriend (a fierce looking guy) believed in Jesus. They took communion which is forbidden for a communist party member. The policewoman's boyfriend, Lau, said to me, "I never experienced so much love like I have in this place."

On May 9, we had a government official join the meeting. He drove up and left in a black Audi. I was concerned that we were going to be arrested that night, but the Lord protected us. Gordon Robertson, the son of PTL's Pat Robertson, was with me. He shared a tremendous message about faith. Afterwards, three people were baptized in the Holy Spirit and spoke in tongues.

On May 16, I was even more concerned that we would be arrested. Before the meeting, there were extremely loud booms of thunder. After a while the thunder stopped. We had no problems. When this happened, I remembered how when the Philistines planned an attack on Israel, God made it thunder loudly. "While Samuel was sacrificing the burnt offering, the Philistines drew near to engage Israel in battle. But that day the Lord thundered

191

with loud thunder against the Philistines and threw them into such a panic that they were routed before the Israelites."

On May 23, we were informed that the PSB knew that we had "Jesus Meetings" in the home of Joseph. We needed a larger room. We planned to move our meeting to a new location. The gates of hell shall not prevail against the Church of Christ.

Over 18 tons of Bibles were transferred into the hands of believers in the PRC during May. More Bibles were moved after Li Peng threatened action. By God's grace, His people prevailed.

Mercy was two. Sherry's desire to accompany me on trips to Guangzhou increased. She enjoyed the ministry to children at the Zhiling school. The children and Sherry made two trips this month with our mission team.

Another man in Guangzhou had a vision of Jesus. He was sick in bed until the Lord appeared to him. Jesus healed him. Glory to God!

A man once told us that he had a vision of Jesus, Sherry, and me with many children. On our 12th Wedding Anniversary (June 5), the Lord opened the door for us to visit an orphanage called, "The Guangzhou Social Children's Welfare Institution. It was in the Tian He District. There were 350 orphans. Most of the orphans had special needs. We were shown two wings of the facility that were recently renovated. The babies and children were in bad shape. Some had horrendous sores on their heads and bodies. I saw one baby with flies crawling in its mouth and nose. Another had an eye bulging out of the socket due to an infection.

Surviving their illnesses was the major concern of these children. Some only stared into space despondently, while others greeted us happily with arms outstretched for love.

This orphanage was run by the Department of Social Welfare and Relief, Guangzhou Civil Administration Bureau. The Deputy Director of this government department was Mrs. Xu Chi. She met with us over breakfast and told us of the many financial needs that this department had. Our goal was to bring volunteers once per week to give the babies baths, pray for them and to speak God's Word to the older ones.

Our second trip to Guangzhou included a visit to the Zhiling school. Glory sang Christian songs there to the special needs teenagers. They clapped and jumped with excitement.

We rented a large hall in a hotel that was equipped with a public-address system and a stage for our evening service. 11 HK Christians assisted with this meeting. Four students from RCC's student fellowship led the worship, one of which was our friend Happy. The older Christians played instruments, shared testimonies, Scriptures, and a message. Grace, Glory, Andrew, and Sherry sang, shared testimonies, and did a skit. Two newcomers believed in Christ. We praise God for His grace.

In June, Adria Star came to HK. She and her husband Stephen had 10 children. They had a family ministry called the Star Family Singers. They had a television program called, "Hide the Word in Your Heart Club." Their programs helped parents and children to memorize Scripture verses. Their oldest son, Paul, had memorized the entire Gospel of Mark, First – Second Timothy and Titus. Their youngest, Mercy, at age two, had memorized Psalm 23. Children who memorized a prescribed amount of Bible verses earned a colorful metal badge.

The Star Family gave us 10 different 60-minute videos of their programs. They gave us authority to copy them and to distribute them. A HK Christian lady gave us enough money to purchase video recording equipment. We made 35 videos and distributed them in HK and in the PRC.

Adria and her oldest daughter, Regina, went with me to Guangzhou on July 4. We put on a program at the Zhiling school. After this, Adria shared in the Guangzhou Fellowship about the importance of memorizing Scripture.

Sherry duplicated the Star Family videos while doing housework. Then, distributed them. When Sherry gave the mothers the videos, they tended to share with her about their concerns for their children and she prayed for them. Mothers from the following countries received videos: HK, PRC, US, South Korea, Switzerland, Singapore, Sierra Leone, and Japan. Many children memorized Bible verses.

Last Monday was my sixth trip to visit the Guangzhou orphans. In the beginning, I was not welcomed warmly, but as Christians prayed, claimed Scripture promises and gave love offerings, the Vice-Director of the orphanage began to greet me kindly. On August 29, he gave me permission to start bringing teams of volunteers into the orphanage.

During our last visit, the toddlers lined up to have their faces washed. Some wanted their heads, arms and bodies washed. When I asked one boy if he wanted to play toys with me, he replied, "No" and hugged me tighter. He only wanted to be held. We held two and three babies at a time on our laps.

During the last three visits, we encouraged a 14-year-old boy named Ho Siu Ngon. He was wheelchair bound. He had a Bible. He read it to the children.

Grace, Glory and Andrew started joining the Sunday school class at RCC for Chinese speaking children. Grace and Glory learned to sing songs in Chinese. They befriended the Chinese children.

Grace and Glory sang two songs in Cantonese this month at Bethel Chapel in Sheung Shui district. This was during a VBS class. They also sang at the Wailing Center in Guangzhou. Lilian, their friend accompanied their singing at Wailing, as did a young man named Aaron Star. Aaron is the fourth child among the Star Family's 10 children. Several students at Wailing gave their lives to Jesus. During our evening meeting, people sat in rooms adjacent to the living room and stood in the doorway. There was not enough room in the large living room for everyone.

During our return train trip from Guangzhou, Aaron played his guitar, and our team sang Christian songs in Cantonese. The train was delayed two hours along the way. There was no air conditioning. It was hot, humid, and uncomfortable. But our team members praised Jesus with joy given to us by the Holy Spirit.

The Star Family gave us their puppet stage, puppets, and sound tracts. Grace, Glory and Andrew practiced puppet skits. They planned to do Gospel skits for guests in the future.

Our sister in Christ, Veronica Luk, began to work at Zhiling school full-time. Veronica willingly left the comforts and conveniences of HK to work in Guangzhou. We introduced Veronica to the staff members of the school.

During September, I wrote, "At the orphanage, we sensed the presence of the God who cares for the fatherless. As I washed one orphan's face, the verse came to me, 'He will wipe every tear from their eyes. There will be no more death or mourning or crying or pain, for the old order of things has passed away.' [27] The dirt on the baby's face reminded me of the shortcomings of humanity. But the joy of the moment was that I felt a tremendous love from God for him, and a desire, even a delight, to change his dirt to cleanliness. His despair to joy! Very soon our Abba Father will take us up in His everlasting arms and take away the remembrance of former tragedies, abuses, and reproaches. Only joy and fellowship in our Father's house shall remain.

Rice porridge was served to the orphans from a bucket. Due to insufficient bowls and spoons, some used the dirty utensils of others. They wore rags. They were thin and dehydrated. Their teeth were black. One small boy was chained with a lock to his crib. The cribs had bamboo mats for mattresses on wooden

---

[27] Revelation 21:4

boards. It was dusty and drafty in the room. Diapers were seldom changed. Their wounded skin struggled to shield them from sickness. Some cribs lacked sidebars. The floor was grey cement. A deaf child pouted face down on the floor. Twice, volunteers witnessed dead children being removed from the room.

Most of these babies were left on a doorstep of a hospital or at a police station. Most had physical defects. God loved them. In God's eyes gratitude is beautiful. They were grateful."

During September, Sherry and the children joined me on two out of three of my orphanage visits. Our children looked forward to these trips. Grace offered Bible stories. 10 of the children were happy to sit and listen to her share. Sherry said to me, "We must share the Gospel with these children because we don't know if we will see them again."

During the last trip, Gavin Campbell from South Africa joined us. He was an evangelist who helped South African orphans and Mozambique refugees. Pastor Francis Lim from Singapore joined our ministry team. He had just come from a 15-day mission to tribal people in the Philippines. Edith Verhagen from Holland, Denise Roff from Ireland and a nurse from England were a part of our mission team as well. They came to HK to take Bibles to the PRC, but when they heard about our orphanage ministry, they wanted to be a part of it as well.

A Christian worker at the orphanage told us how the officials persecuted her. She wept often. During her first year at the orphanage, she only saw one child believe in Christ. During,

197

the second year, eight more children believed in Christ. She held a weekly prayer meeting with them. I believe God had opened this door for us via her prayers. The Christian children were standouts due to their benevolent natures.

CCLC in HK gave us three large bags of children's Christian literature and cassette tapes. Sister Edith Verhaegen brought the items safely across the border. A portion of these items went to Zhiling school and the other portion to the orphans.

A Taiwanese family donated $1,500 to help the orphans. We used these funds to pay the costs of bringing volunteers from HK to the Guangzhou. We needed more hands and hearts to care for these children. The volunteers helped us to bring boxes of fruits and toys from HK to Guangzhou.

On September 4, at 8:42 pm, the home in which we were meeting was surrounded by police cars and officers. Nobody panicked! I had memorized Psalm 3 on the way to Guangzhou that day. I stood up and recited the entire Psalm in Cantonese. For over an hour, the police surrounded us, but they did not knock on the door. Finally, we dismissed everyone. The police had left. The house next door had been robbed. If the police had knocked on our door earlier, they would have found a living room packed with people, hymnals, and Bibles.

The next week, about 500 soldiers were marching on the street near to the same home. Our taxi had to drive up on the sidewalk to pass by them. The Lord watched over us.

Lemuel began to lead the Guangzhou Fellowship. On September 18, we began to rent a room in a restaurant that could hold 50 people. I rented this room so that if we were arrested by the PSB, I could take the blame for organizing the meeting and ask the PSB to release the attendees.

Sherry duplicated and distributed 180 Star Family videos to promote Scripture memorization and family ministry. We distributed the videos in HK and in the PRC. We mailed some to people in the Philippines and South Africa.

On November 1, I wrote, "Since August, I have been teaching a foundational Bible study for young teenagers. I also taught a course on evangelism during the last two months. I am now teaching in Cantonese. My curriculum is in Chinese. I translate the lesson into English to ensure that I know what every word means. I practice pronouncing the words. Emmanuel (God with us) gives me the victory."

Sherry, the children, and I practiced a Christmas program with the Sunday school children. There were over 60 children in the class. We practiced five Christmas songs in Cantonese, as well as skits. Sherry made outfits for the children.

Two members of the Guangzhou fellowship joined our outreach to the orphans. During our last visit, a nurse named Mrs. Yang told us that she had only ate one meal per day during the last two weeks. During this time, the Holy Spirit filled her. She spoke in tongues. She is an older lady. Her fellow Christians don't believe in this gift. The Holy Spirit gave her the gift anyway.

On December 2, I wrote, "A Marxist has come to Christ. Before he believed in Christ two months ago, Mr. Ng was beating his sister and mother. He blasphemed God and praised Marxism. Now, he thanks us for preaching Christ to him. His testimony is, 'Jesus is good.' His mother and sister have attended our meetings for more than a year now. They recognize that his conversion is a miracle of God."

On November 20, our family assisted Mercy and Yu Zhung with their wedding ceremony. Our children were in the procession. Mercy asked me to officiate. Unbeknownst to me there were sailors present. Besides teaching on the meaning of marriage, the Lord led me to share the salvation message.

A few weeks ago, a Sister Violet Kiteley from Shiloh Christian Fellowship shared at a meeting. During the meeting, a security guard in uniform entered the meeting room with a walkie talkie in hand. As Sister Kiteley spoke, the guard left and did not return. She spoke on the spirit of Elijah. She spoke about how God divinely protected a group of missionaries from being killed by the communists in the early 40's. That night, the Holy Spirit filled four people. Thanks be to God for His grace.

Three Sundays ago, Pastor Dennis shared with us a video of a house church in northern China. There were 5,000 Christians gathered in a field fervently worshipping God. They carried a wooden cross and sang praises to Jesus Christ for saving them. There was also a scene of a five-year-old boy standing on a stool and boldly preaching the Gospel to a room full of listening adults.

A team of New Zealanders bought new metal bowls and spoons for the orphans. This was a costly contribution because there were so many orphans. Many of their old metal bowls were rusty, dented, and chipped.

The Lord blessed me to be able give a Christian nurse a bag full of books about the baptism of the Holy Spirit. She gave everyone in her house group one of these books including her pastor. Their response was, "We want more."

I brought teams of volunteers to the orphanage on a weekly basis. We did three hours of service per week. Afterwards, I put the volunteers on a train back to HK. I stayed in Guangzhou. I met up with Lemuel for the house church meeting. For those who wanted to do long-term and full-time orphanage ministry, I referred them to Moses Vegh. Moses was the China representative for the James Robison orphan ministry.

On December 15, I wrote Sherry's parents, "Sherry is a tremendous blessing to my life. I love her. She is doing great as a mother of four children on the mission field. She holds the babies of other mothers on Sundays. She holds baby Mercy Ngo (the daughter of Steve and Mai). Chinese ladies give her clothes to distribute to the missionary children. She also holds the African babies. She provides special care to a Singaporean mother of four children. She has been caring for the daughter of Peggy Knosp for a few weeks now. Peggy has lung cancer."

"Grace and Glory are worshippers of God. They do worship dance to the Lord during Sunday services. ABC News was here last Sunday. They televised a portion of the worship service in which they were dancing. They are doing well in school. They help us around the house. Andrew makes gifts for us, for his sisters, for others and for his teacher. He is an explorer. He likes to collect grasshoppers, lizards, fish, snails, precious stones and just about anything else that can be found outside. Mercy is loving. She loves to be around her Dad. She gives me kisses and likes me to read her Bible stories. She loves to play dolls, to watch Christian videos and to play at the park. She knows most of Psalm 23 by memory. Grace, Glory and Andrew have memorized many verses of the Bible. They pray for others."

On December 22, a HK company donated $650 worth of new and unused toys for the orphans. Seven huge boxes full of toys! They also gave $94 in cash. So, the day after Christmas, at 7:40 am, my family, Glenn and Rheba Carter, Paul and Kim Ryan, and three HK Christians pulled seven boxes on five luggage carts from Fanling village to the train station. When we arrived at the orphanage, we were excited to distribute the toys, but the authorities stopped us. We prayed. Then, they changed their minds and allowed the gift-giving to proceed. The children were happy. The children ran to us from every direction. It did not take long to distribute the toys.

During December, we began to sponsor the expenses of one orphan named Chan Ling. We watched to see if his condition improved due to our monthly sponsorship of $20. We did not see any improvement during December.

The caregivers at the orphanage did not seem to think of the children as human beings. Laundry was placed on shelves before it was dry. Diapers were seldom changed. A pair of two-year-old toddlers slept under their cribs on the concrete floor. One baby had blood and pus oozing out its ear. Her pain was great. Sherry shooed mosquitos and bugs off babies. We saw a supply truck arrive one day. Bags of rice and bottles of cooking oil were unloaded for the orphans. However, when we rode the day-staff's bus back to the city, the workers had the bags of rice and bottles of cooking oil among their things. The children were hungry. Gifts that we brought to the children disappeared. We prayed for an end to the injustice but continued to give.

Last November, a Sister Judy Duly and a team of people from her church in New Zealand, went to the orphanage with me. After they returned to New Zealand, she gave me a call to tell me that her church was praying for this ministry. She also told me that many sisters in the church were sewing clothes for the children. She asked them to pray over the material and for the children while they sewed the outfits.

The babies and children needed socks and shoes. They had none. YWAM donated new shirts and pants to help clothe them.

The Lord gave us favor with the authorities. The Deputy Director of Social Welfare in Guangzhou, Mrs. Xu Chi, gave us permission to take photos of the orphans receiving our gifts. Mr. Zheng Men Chun, the Vice Head of the Institute treated us roughly, but after we responded to him with kindness, his demeanor changed. Sometimes, he conversed with uniformed officials. On one such occasion, I offered to shake the official's hand. I spoke to him in Mandarin. He brightened up.

One day, the authorities presented to me a certificate with a red velvet cover. They thanked me for having a loving heart. Later, I used this award as proof to border guards that I was transporting goods into the PRC for orphans and not selling them for profit. This way, they did not charge me customs duty.

Two weeks ago, I met a university professor with her 30 students. She started a conversation with me. At first, I assumed she was a concerned medical professor who was teaching her students how to care for orphans. To my absolute horror, I discovered she was a professor of eugenics. Eugenics is a Nazi-Germany type policy. This practice eliminates unwanted babies by means of forced abortion and sterilization. She used the miserable conditions of these children to support the lie that eugenics is a good policy. I said to her and to her students, "Eugenics is like Hitler's master race plan. It is full of hypocrisy because there is no perfect person. Who has the right to judge whether someone should live or die; or be able to have children or to be sterilized? Beautiful and intelligent people have also caused great havoc and destruction to people." I did not mention Mao Zedong, Lenin, or Stalin as examples of mass murderers. She responded, "We must be on our way. Goodbye!"

Adoption was expensive. The US Embassy had a list of approved adoptions agencies. Lifelink was one. The cost to adopt one of these babies was $9,000. $3,000 to the orphanage! $1,000 to the communist party! $2,500 to transit the baby through HK to another country! $2,500 to the US agency.

We distributed Gospel tracts to the orphans. We took note of their challenges. Yuet Jing, an eight-year-old girl, believed in Jesus. She had heart surgery. Hoi Ding was missing a thigh bone in her leg. Ah-Chee had an enlarged heart and poor blood circulation. He missed meals because he could not wake up in time to eat. Chan Ling had deformed legs and a deformed back. Taan Fa sat on the floor and cried. Her wheelchair needed repaired. She refused to eat lunch. After I mentioned this to the staff, they repaired her chair and brought it to her immediately. Then, she was happy. Taan Fa was a Christian.

Four assistant teachers at Wailing Kindergarten believed in Jesus during a December 26 meeting. Grace, Glory and Andrew sang in Cantonese at this meeting. On December 27, they also sang at the Wailing Kindergarten for the students of Veronica. Veronica had her students sing the Christmas songs in English that she taught them. Her students told us the Christmas story in English. Later, when I asked them, "How many of you believed in Jesus?" Every one of them raised their hands and said that they did. God has mightily used Veronica in their lives.

On Christmas Day, Grace and Glory sang and recited Scriptures with her Sunday school class children in front of the church congregation. During the second service, four HK students, whom I discipled using a "New Life Foundations – First

Stage" booklet, were baptized. A fifth student that Happy led to Jesus was also baptized. Between 2-4 pm, our children did a puppet show in the park. They helped distribute Gospel tracts while singers from our church sang. During the Christmas dinner at our church, Grace and Glory sang and recited Psalms chapters one, eight and twenty-three. Andrew and Mercy were also involved in some of the songs and Scripture recitation. They received Christmas gifts from those to whom they sang.

~ Chapter 12 ~
Called by the Gospel (1995)

On January 28, Pastor Dennis made establishing small study groups a priority for 1995. I coordinated, managed finances and did reporting for the Guangzhou small group ministry. I had leaders for two small groups and was endeavoring to recruit a third pair of leaders for a third small group.

On January 12, Pastor Dennis directed Evangelist Reinhard Bonnke to me so that he could share with Guangzhou Christians. Bonnke held large crusades in 33 nations of Africa. His meetings often exceeded 100,000 people in attendance. God did special miracles during his crusades.

He preached in every major city of Rwanda just before the massacre took place. Nearly 10,000 people converted to Christ in every city where he preached. Glory to God!

We had just over 60 people present at our Bonnke meeting. He preached from Mark 16:14-16 about being believing believers. The room was packed. Mr. Bonnke had to walk on the seats of the chairs to lay hands on and pray for everyone in the room. People were filled with the Holy Spirit. Praise the Lord!

On January 9 – 11, Dr. Frank Cooksey, his wife Val, and his receptionist Linda, accompanied me to the orphanage. They did examinations and produced medicines for over 100 children. Dr. Cooksey reported that some children had been exposed to atomic radiation, insecticides, and pesticides. He found symptoms of such exposure among them. He noted that one baby's hand had been gnawed by a rat. The orphanage workers explained that when it is cold outside rats come in from outside and crawl into the baby beds to keep warm and sometimes eat on the babies.

On January 16, two Australians and two Americans helped me to take 920 bottles of pre-made baby milk by Nestle to the orphanage. We used five two-wheeled carts to transport 46 cases. This product was donated by Mother's Choice of HK. We were able to conduct a brief worship service with a small group of children. While we were there, we noticed medical workers taking blood samples from the necks of babies using hypodermic needles. "Lord, have mercy!"

On January 23, four members of RCMI's training center volunteered to serve the orphans. One of the members bought a case of apples for the children, another bought a case of drinks and still another a bag of candy for them. I brought blessings from our HK pediatrician. Dr. Chan donated cases of vitamins, a bag full of Desitin diaper cream packets, a small box of Daiperene tubes, medicine cups and spoons, medicine applicators, and baby milk powder. Mother's Choice donated bars of soap, rubber gloves and four more cases of Nestle's baby milk. We worshipped the Lord together with the older children. While there, we met a PRC lady who had adopted a six-week-old baby for just $650.

The PRC recently passed a eugenics law to abort defective fetuses and to sterilize adults likely to give birth to such babies. Evangelist Bonnke said that Hitler had passed a similar eugenics

208

law just before he began "the final solution." He added, "The whole thing sped out of control very fast."

The PRC's leader Deng Xiao Ping suffered with Parkinson Disease. Doctors predicted that he would only last until June. Jiang Zhe Ming was scheduled to become the next leader. We prayed that he would not continue the promotion of eugenics.

Karena led a former army soldier to profess faith in Christ on February 13. He said to Karena, "When I was a soldier, I was not permitted to believe in Christ, but now I can." This man joined the fellowship meetings on several occasions before he professed faith in Christ. Karena had taken note of him at the end of one fellowship meeting. She asked him questions about his relationship with God, and then, encouraged him to call upon the Name of the Lord. The Lord also used Karena on February 20 to lead a visitor to faith in Jesus.

The Guangzhou Fellowship South averaged between 30-40 in attendance. The Guangzhou Fellowship North was attended by seven during their first meeting. Producing disciples that produced more disciples was our goal. James was a success story. He went on a long trip to several cities in northern China during the Chinese New Year holiday. He preached the Gospel to many people during that trip.

James had an office with a computer, fax machine and telephone. He offered to let me use his office space for my operations. In addition to the help of James, Stephen helped me serve the orphans.

Mother's Choice, a branch of YWAM, donated shoes and socks for the orphans. The children now had ample shoes, but sadly, tended to take them off. Our family's doctor donated more than 40 cans of powdered baby milk and over 150 packets of baby cereal. His nurses gave $75 for the orphans. We took clothes and food to the children. Spiritually, our team led 20 orphans to profess faith in Jesus.

On March 20, Sherry, the children, and I, together with volunteers from Mother's Choice, transported 12 orphans to the Guangzhou Zoo. A Christian nurse accompanied our entourage. She led the children to sing praise songs to Jesus. The children were exceedingly happy. Two HK sisters helped us. Three from the Guangzhou Fellowship helped us. Glory to God!

On March 27, Brother Ralph Mahoney, Director of World M.A.P. and his wife Gretchen, as well as a 77-year-old pastor named Paul Peterson and his wife Virginia joined us in serving the orphans. The children were grateful for their attention and prayers. Brother Mahoney taught the disciples from his newly translated book entitled, "The Shepherd's Staff." 70 of us were packed into the meeting room. He taught the Paul-to-Timothy discipleship method. Each member was to find a faithful person with whom they could share what they knew about Jesus. If each member discipled one new person per year, then, the church would double in size each year. He shared about the fruits of the Spirit (having Christ's character) and on the gifts of the Spirit (having Christ's ability). Praise the Lord!

Feeling emboldened by our progress with the orphans and the orphanage staff, I applied for permission with the Guangzhou government to start an association entitled, "The Mercy Charitable Association." Ironically, I was grateful when the officials discouraged me from trying to become a legal entity. They explained that recognition by the government would cause me more trouble than help. They did offer me a desk in their social welfare office from which I could continue to build our social service ministry. They said I could hire staff and move my family to Guangzhou. It sounded great, but I did not want to do another ministry behind the government's back, especially inside a government building. If these officials were doing things behind their superiors' backs, what would they do behind my back?

On April 10, the Lord arranged a concert in Guangzhou City at the Ramada Inn for our Christian contacts there. The original agreement that I had with the hotel was for a room that could hold 100 people for just under $50, but on the night of the concert, we were given a room that could hold 300 people for the same price. Nearly 100 Chinese attended the concert. 40 guests from overseas were present. The Celebrant Singers led us with music and singing. Jesus was exalted! Moses Vegh shared the message. 30 people came forward for prayer. Some were weeping with their faces to the floor. Nine people believed in Jesus. Seven people were filled with the Holy Spirit. One man said that he experienced the presence of the Holy Spirit like electricity filling him. Praise the Lord! God is wonderful.

The Celebrant Singers sang to 50 of the orphans at the orphanage. Some cried tears of joy because the Holy Spirit had so touched their hearts. The Singers danced with the children. They invited some on the stage with them. They played with the children. The children felt loved.

Two sisters from Mother's Choice planned to move near to the orphanage and serve them. I advised them on places to live, transportation routes and where to buy groceries. I also mediated between them and the orphanage directors.

Sherry had children's meetings in our home. Usually, 8-10 children attended. The children worshiped the Lord and memorized Scriptures. Praise be to God for this!

Several Christian leaders were arrested in Guangzhou. A Brother Li was severely beaten. Lemuel and I met with the fellowship leaders on May 8. A fellowship member informed us that a government raid on our weekly meeting was imminent. At first, a spirit of fear prevailed among them, but as we shared Scriptures and emphasized the importance of the Gospel ministry, God gave them faith to move forward.

One member took us to hotel where there was a meeting room that we could rent for $70 per month cheaper than our current location. The new location held 70 to 80 people. This new meeting room was available during the early evening hours whereas the old one could only be used from 9 pm until midnight. God turned a bad situation into a good one.

Peter, our most likely local candidate to take over the pastoral work in Guangzhou announced his resignation from the group. He wanted members to telephone him to find out where the next meeting would be. We disagreed because the government monitored telephone conversations. A major crackdown on Christianity was happening. We wanted to release the 70 disciples into the care of a local leader but did not have peace to do so.

A missionary friend of Sherry's named Peggy Knosp went to be with Jesus on April 21, at 4:05 pm. Peggy had cancer. Sherry missed her greatly. Peggy's daughter, Mandy, often ministered in music together with Grace and Glory. Our hearts were especially burdened for Mandy.

On May 26, I wrote, "Sherry has been leading our children and the children of their school to sing Scripture songs. The Lord laid it on her heart to start a "Hide the Word in Your Heart Club" in our home on Mondays while I am in China. The children memorized Scriptures, prayed for one another, shared testimonies, and learned new songs. As the children hid God's Word in their hearts, the Lord brought forth good fruit in their lives.

Happy took 40 students to a Christian camp. She shared the Gospel with these students. 35 of these 40 students believed in Jesus. Happy was happy. Just nine years earlier at this camp, she met Sherry's sister Louise. Happy believed in Jesus via the efforts of Louise, Sherry, and others.

Concerning Lily and Yan Chi, we supported their rent and living expenses at the rate of $210 per month. Lily started a clothing business and earned some money. We planned to keep supporting her until September to ensure that her and the baby did not starve. Lily hosted a Bible study in her apartment for three months. A missionary named Keith baptized four of the converts.

On May 22, a minister from Wenzhou shared with our fellowship. He had seen many miracles while serving Jesus for 19-years. Once, when he was imprisoned for preaching the Gospel, an angel set him free. Once, when he preached in Mongolia, the Lord caused the sun to melt the ice over a frozen river in time for a baptism service. This minister stayed with a Christian whose family members were Buddhist. Before he arrived, their business barely made money, but on the day that he arrived, they made $930 in one day. In Wenzhou, 10% of its six million people were Christians. It was a prosperous city. The Wenzhou Christians sent missionaries to many regions of the PRC. He explained to our fellowship members the four reasons why the government set up the Three-self Patriotic Movement churches. The four reasons were to gather, exploit, control, and to destroy Christians.

Concerning the orphanage, nine members of a small Christian group in HK volunteered to help our family take 12 orphans to the Guangzhou Zoo. The Lord especially used William and Joyce to make this trip a success.

Hillary from Mother's Choice served the entire day on May 22 at the orphanage. She said that while she was there the workers did their jobs. Thankfully, the director welcomed more volunteers to help. Hillary said that one-day of work there was extremely exhausting.

The Lord healed a baby whose head was swollen in many places. She looked as though she would die soon. After prayer, her head healed quickly. Only one small bump remained on her forehead. The orphanage nurse testified that it was a miracle. We prayed for God to heal Ho Sui Kam, Taan Fa and Yuet Jing. Their dormitory was infected with hepatitis. They were infected.

The phone rang on the evening of June 10. It was Veronica from Guangzhou. A university authority had tipped her off that the police planned to arrest Lemuel and me on Monday (June 12). Grace and Glory cried when they heard this news. They, along with Andrew, begged me not to go to the PRC. Sherry committed me into God's hands. By faith, I told Andrew in the presence of Grace and Glory, "The police won't catch me, I will catch them."

Lemuel and I were not arrested. We had a surprise guest speaker! It was Brother Yun who was widely known as the Heavenly Man. His story is told in the book entitled, "Lilies Amongst Thorns." He was incarcerated for four years for preaching the Gospel. He was punched, kicked, urinated on, and stung with electric cattle prods. Despite mistreatment, he continued to witness to those in prison. Many believed in Christ. Having done without a Bible for four years, when Brother Yun received one, he read the whole Bible through and memorized 55 chapters within a 90-day period.

One 17-year-old believed in Jesus after listening to his preaching. When the meeting ended, an army jeep was near the courtyard gate. Soldiers stood around it. Though they watched us, we had peace. We continued to fellowship in Jesus unphased by their presence. After 45-minutes the soldiers left. God's presence was greater than the presence of His enemies. Brother Yun stayed with Lemuel and me that evening.

When I told Brother Yun that my children had memorized many Bible verses, he was happy. He told the Christians that he extremely supported our ministry to the orphans. He emphasized that God is the God of the orphan.

On June 12, the same day that we met Brother Yun, 23 student traffic police did mandatory service at the orphanage. They cut the grass with scissor like cutters. They were being disciplined. The Lord gave me favor in their eyes. I led them into the baby room and urged them to hold the babies. They became happy and friendly. They asked me if they could take a group picture with me. I said yes on the condition that I could have a picture of me with them using my camera. In this way, God fulfilled the word that the Lord gave me to tell my children. I caught the police by way of my camera. Glory to God!

Due to the threats of arrest that began in early May, we moved our meeting point from a restaurant to a believer's home. Then, we were warned to leave there. Next, the Lord led us to meet in a center for the handicapped where four of our members lived. We had glorious meetings there. As Isaiah 35 says, the Lord

216

caused a rose to bloom in the wilderness. In the most unlikely place, God's work flourished. On June 26, I shared the testimony of Michael Edmond of Columbia, Missouri. Michael was shot four times and ended up paralyzed from the waist down. Later, he was born again. Since then, he has preached the Gospel to many. The handicapped Christians were encouraged by his testimony.

On June 12, Mr. Zhang, the orphanage director denied our team of 42 people entry. On June 26, the health director, Mrs. Leung, told me that his words not only applied to the 42 people, but also included me. She urged me to find orphans in HK or America to help. She told me that if I wanted to revisit, I would have to receive approval from higher authorities. A Christian nurse told Veronica that this new restriction was the result of a TV documentary that was produced in Britain and broadcasted throughout Europe. The documentary showed visual abuses of children at the Guangzhou orphanage. Since then, foreign volunteers were denied entrance. Adoptions to foreigners were halted. A Chinese delegation cancelled their trip to Sweden due to this orphan documentary being shown there. I planned to visit the higher authorities on July 3 to request permission to reenter.

On June 14, members of the Hide the Word in Your Heart Club started weekly morning prayer meetings. They planned to soon start a meeting in Fanling Wai for unbelieving children. Missionary children would lead these meetings with the help of Sherry and Helen.

On July 1, Mary, Luther, Helen, and Sherry began a meeting for unbelieving village children. Eight HK children attended the first meeting. 14 HK children attended the second and third meeting. Grace, Glory, Lilian, Gu Yan, and Ho Yan taught Bible stories. They taught how to worship God with song, dance, hand gestures and joy. The attendees enjoyed it.

The PRC has set up a giant clock at the border to count down the days, hours, and seconds before it takes possession of HK from Britain. There were 700 days or 61 million seconds remaining before the takeover. Many locals planned to move out of HK before the PRC takes over.

On July 3, the authorities at the center for the handicapped stopped our meeting and told us to leave. We had met in the courtyard there for a month. Veronica and Sister Huang led a meeting just down the street, so we joined with them. On July 10, Christians from the handicapped center assured me that no harm came to them from our holding meetings at their center.

Mr. Ho believed in Jesus on July 3. His wife and Veronica broke up the idols and tore down the family idol shelf at his request. He had liver disease. Lemuel and I shared God's promises about divine healing with him. He needed $25,000 for a transplant. His work unit would not pay for his operation.

Mrs. Hau lived in a four-room apartment. Two rooms served as a snack shop and their bedroom. The kitchen floor and bathroom floor only had enough room for one person to stand in. They had boxes of goods stacked up inside the bedroom. Their

17-year-old son slept on a shelf-like bed near the ceiling. They worked from 8 am until 1 am. They barely made enough money to survive. Despite her poverty, she brought a visitor to our meeting almost every week. She brought four first-time guests on July 24. She is an example of James 2:5: "The Lord has chosen the poor of this world to be rich in faith, and heirs of the kingdom which He has promised to them that love Him."

The Lord led me to help Mike Francen get one of his books, "A Miracle Settles the Issue" translated into Chinese. A testimony by Michael Edmonds was translated into a tract. We duplicated 30 cassettes of Scriptures, children's Bible stories and Scripture songs for distribution in the PRC. We distributed Star Family videos to promote Scripture memorization. I enlarged the print in the Star Family's Scripture memorization book.

On July 10, we gave $1,762.50 to the proper government officers (Dr. Chen and Mrs. Zhang) for the support of orphans. The donors requested that we do this. The Chinese leaders urged me to return next week to speak with the Deputy Director of Social Service Welfare. They gave me an application to complete. On the application, I requested permission to bring teams of 12 people or less per week into the orphanage for 12 months.

On July 23, Veronica called from Guangzhou and told Sherry, "The PSB are looking for whole groups of Christians to arrest. They want to make a public example of one or two foreigners." An elderly sister shared this info with Veronica. We sought the Lord. Other faithful friends prayed too. Then, at our

July 24 Guangzhou meeting, we had five new guests and a Mr. Tam believed in Jesus. It was a wonderful meeting. No police showed up. JESUS protected us!

Veronica moved north to teach about 300 children in an underground church. Concerning Lily, we extended her support to include this month and the next but reduced her support from $225 to $125. She was grateful for the $125 because she had prepared to do without any support after June. She became an Amway distributor and held Christian meetings in her home. Veronica stayed with Lily a few days. She confirmed that Lily had sufficient finances.

I am grateful to God for Sherry. The Lord used her mightily in my life. She feared the Lord and sought to please Him. She taught our children and the children of others to pray, worship, memorize Scripture and serve the Lord. She suffered a great deal while in HK but remained a wonderful blessing.

Sister Liza invited Grace and Glory to be a part of the worship dance team at church. They also attended a course on worship. The Lord touched their hearts to worship Him daily.

Sherry coordinated the Hide the Word in Your Heart Club in our home. Grace earned nine Bible memorization badges, Glory ten, Andrew two and Sherry ten. Other members had memorized one to two badges each. One of the HK girls told Sherry, "Thank you for all you have done for us."

Sherry and I were non-paid volunteers at RCC. I was on the board of elders and deacons. I preached during a Sunday service. I led prayer meetings, fellowship meetings, cell group meetings and helped with evangelistic outreaches. Recently, I preached a message entitled, "Wholehearted Worshippers." One New Zealander told me that she was singing praises to the Lord in an elevator after that message and the Lord opened the door for her to witness to someone for over an hour. I shared in a cell group of young adults a message entitled, "Roses Blooming in the Wilderness" from Isaiah 35:1, 6. Afterwards, the cell group members decided to take-action to help the Guangzhou orphans.

On August 7, I went to Guangzhou alone. I was on a high-risk mission. I went to the Provincial Government Headquarters of Guangdong Province to request permission to continue the ministry into the orphanage. When I arrived at the Tian He train station, I stopped at a refreshment stand to get a drink. As I gulped a drink down, I noticed to my side, a boy standing near me. He was a beggar. I thought he wanted me to give him my empty can for recycling purposes, so I gave it to him. He lifted the can to his mouth to drink the last drop. At that moment, the Lord spoke to my heart. He said, "This is why you are going to the provincial headquarters today. You are going to advocate for children like this one." The Lord turned my heart away from concerns about me to concerns about the orphans. A taxi pulled up. I gave him the address. I had resolve to carry out my mission.

I met with Mrs. Zhan Xiu Lan concerning my desire to continue serving the orphans. Mrs. Zhan was the section Chief of Foreign Affairs, Guangdong Provincial Civil Affairs Bureau. An armed guard was posted in the room while I spoke with her. She gave me permission to speak freely. I told her that my goal was to bring love and care to the orphans. I wanted to train HK and western Christians to die to themselves and to render care to those who were in worse condition than themselves. I told her that this was the example of Jesus. "He left heaven to come down to earth for the benefit and salvation of others."

Mrs. Zhan glowed as the Lord touched her heart. She thanked me. She requested an official letter in Chinese concerning my background and purpose. She promised to see what she could do to get me back in the orphanage. That official letter was hand delivered to her on August 28. On August 29, Mrs. Zhan called to RCC and asked the secretary, Sybil, to tell me that I was granted permission to continue bringing teams of 12 people or less on a weekly basis to the orphanage. This good news was waiting for me when I got back to HK. Glory to God!

Some of our Guangzhou Fellowship members were active locally and others nationwide in witnessing for Jesus. A taxi driver in the group handed out Gospel tracts to his passengers and witnessed to them. One brother named Peter went to Qinghai Province and joined the house church movement there.

Peter, his wife and daughter saw with their own eyes a resurrection from the dead. While standing in a church doorway, an old man suddenly fell over dead. His breathing stopped. The Christians gathered around and prayed for him. His life was restored. He was totally healed. Peter heard the testimony of a paralytic woman whom Jesus healed. This woman had a dream in which she was trying to touch the garment of Jesus. Her husband said that she cried for two hours in her sleep. Then, suddenly, in the dream she touched the garment of Jesus, woke up and was instantly healed. Many believed in Jesus because of this miracle. A little boy with mumps was instantly healed after Christians prayed for him. After seeing and hearing these miracles, Peter asked Jesus to heal his wife, daughter, and himself because they became sick during the trip. Jesus also healed them instantly.

Peter had been a member of the Three-self Church movement for many years. This church taught him to oppose those who believe in miracles, cast out demons and speak in tongues. Now, that he had seen with his own eyes the mighty power of God, he would never be the same. Praise the Lord!

Mary went to Tibet. While there, she heard Christians praying loudly in a Buddhist temple. She went into the temple to investigate and found a group of Christians from RCMI's Tibetan ministry. They were praying in Jesus' Name against the evil spirits of Buddhism that blinded the eyes of most Tibetans. One of the Christians was Katherine Bryant from Life Christian Center in St. Louis, MO. Mary recognized her because I had brought Katherine to Guangzhou previously. They were amazed how the Lord arranged for them to meet in Tibet.

A Pastor Rusty Domingue, director of Russel Domingue Ministries spoke to the fellowship members. Two unbelievers believed in Christ after he preached. Glory to God!

On September 11, many roses bloomed in Guangzhou. More than 120 Chinese gathered to worship the Lord, praise His Name, and give Him thanks. What a beautiful sight it was to see them leap for joy and worship God with gladness of heart. A team of 29 people from Calvary Temple in Irving, Texas, led worship at the Novatel. They brought in 600 Bibles. 10 members of the team visited the orphanage with me. They sang to the orphans, anointed them with oil, prayed for them, loved them, and gave $1,085 in offerings to the orphanage.

The Calvary Temple ministry team also did a street outreach at HK's famous Star Ferry pier. Our entire family participated in this outreach. Sister Kathy met a young man who had lost both his parents, lost his girlfriend and was about to lose his business. She urged me to share with him. I was able to share Scripture and testimonies with him. He professed faith in Christ. His name was David.

The Calvary Temple team also visited an orphanage in HK called Mother's Choice with us. On Sunday evening, David invited Sherry and me, along with other RCC representatives to join their team for a meal on the Jumbo floating boat restaurant. They bought us clothes, toys for our children and gave us an offering to help us out.

Sherry had copied 200 Star Family videos but received more requests. So, we bought an additional case of 100 blank videos. She made an additional 20 copies in response to added requests. Monica Hawkins from Sweden led her two sons to memorize many verses. She promoted the Hide the Word in Your Heart Club at a HK's Women's Aglow meeting. Four mothers at Women's Aglow requested videos in response to her sharing. Kathy Anderson from Switzerland led her two daughters to memorize verses. We sent four videos to a missionary family living in the PRC. Their son enjoyed a previous video that we gave him, so his parents requested more. The Star Family made these videos as a tool to help parents teach their children the Word of God. They gave us permission to copy their videos and share them freely. We did not charge for them.

Sherry showed an excerpt of a Star Family video at a missionary gathering. The excerpt was of the Star Family urging viewers to take Bibles to the PRC. After the video excerpt, Sherry urged everyone to hide God's Word in their hearts. Sherry and the children did this by quoting Bible verses and by singing for them. Sherry shared why memorizing Scripture was a blessing to her.

We thanked God for Maria Tener. She led our village children to memorize Psalm 119:11 within 10 minutes. She made felt award badges to relieve us of the burden of having to purchase parts for medal badges.

On October 6, George and Barbara Ragland prayed in the Name of Jesus for our son Andrew. He had lactose intolerance. In fact, on the evening of October 5, Andrew vomited from drinking too much milk. In recent years, he took pills before eating and drinking so that he could digest the lactose. The Holy Spirit used the Ragland's to heal Andrew. He ate and drank all the milk products he wanted after that. Glory to God!

Maria Tener introduced a new Bible memorization method to the children at our Fanling Wai village meeting. She had a child write a verse on the white board. The children read it. Then, one Chinese character (word) was erased. They tried to recite the entire verse by filling in the missing word via memory. One by one all words were erased, and the children memorized the entire verse. One boy, Ah Chun, told us after the meeting, "This day was the happiest day of my life." Praise the Lord!

On October 2, Lemuel and I had the privilege to baptize seven new believers in a swimming pool in Guangzhou. We rented the whole pool complete with changing rooms for about $35. The Lord also protected us from anti-Christian authorities. On October 20, over 100 Gospel preachers were arrested and imprisoned in Anhui Province. The risk of arrest was real.

On October 23, six New Zealanders, two Brits, one Swiss and three Guangzhou Christians went with me to visit the orphans. The New Zealanders and Brits stayed in Guangzhou until October 31. They did eight hours of voluntary service each day. They did this at their own expense. They used puppets and Christian music to serve them. I arranged transportation and reserved rooms for them near to the orphanage.

A member from David Carpenter's team, Janet Horton, shared on Christian TV in Texas about her trip to the Guangzhou orphanage. Later, she telephoned Sherry to tell her that $1,200 was pledged to support this ministry. This amount added to their previous donation of $1,085. It was enough to purchase two dual purpose heating and air conditioning machines for the baby room in the orphanage. Glory to God!

During April of 1992, I had a dream of a rose blooming. This dream happened three times. The Lord revealed to me that the rose represented people who would bloom for His glory. In May this year, the Lord led me back to Isaiah 35:

>…The desert shall rejoice and blossom as the rose; it shall blossom abundantly and rejoice, even with joy and singing. …They shall see the glory of the Lord, the excellency of our God.
>
>Strengthen the weak hands and make firm the feeble knees. Say to those who are fearful-hearted, 'Be strong, do not fear! Behold, your God will come with vengeance, with the recompense of God; He will come and save you.'
>
>Then the eyes of the blind shall be opened, and the ears of the deaf shall be unstopped. Then the lame shall leap like a deer, and the tongue of the dumb sing. For waters shall burst forth in the wilderness, and streams in the desert. The parched ground shall become a pool, and the thirsty land springs of water; in the habitation of jackals, where each lay, there shall be grass with reeds and rushes.
>
>A highway shall be there, and a road, and it shall be called the Highway of Holiness. The unclean shall not pass over it, but it shall be for others. Whoever walks the road, although a fool, shall not go astray.

227

No lion shall be there, nor shall any ravenous beast go up on it; it shall not be found there. But the redeemed shall walk there, and the ransomed of the Lord shall return, and come to Zion with singing, with everlasting joy on their heads. They shall obtain joy and gladness, and sorrow and sighing shall flee away.

The Guangzhou orphanage was in Lung Dung (Dragon Cave) district. There were many crippled and handicapped children there. A Christian nurse at the orphanage fasted and prayed for two weeks for these children. The Lord gave her a vision of the Holy Spirit giving spiritual gifts to these children. This Dragon Cave had blind, deaf, lame, and mute children. Along the road to this place, there was a monument shop with many vicious looking lions made of stone on display. The dragon and lion are metaphors of the devil in the Bible. The devil did much evil to these orphans. We asked the Lord to deliver these little ones from the dragon and the lion. The Lord did provide streams in this desert. The sorrow and sighing of some did flee away. Some obtained joy and gladness. "O blossom abundantly and rejoice, even with joy and singing children! Behold, the glory of the Lord! Behold, the excellency of our God!"

Crimes happened in broad daylight in Guangzhou. Sister Sandra King had a gun pointed at her head while sitting on a public bus. The gunman was angry at the bus conductor for requesting $0.09 bus fare instead of $0.06, which he declared was the true fare. First, he pointed his gun at the conductor's head and then, at the passengers. Sandra prayed in Jesus' Name that he would put the gun down and he did. He got off the bus. Sandra King volunteered four-days per week at the orphanage.

This month, a gun battle broke out between the police and the army. Many police officers were wounded. A policeman had stopped a soldier. He started to arrest him and impound his car. This was when bullets began to fly.

The Lord provided a HK brother named John from RCC to assist Lemuel with the Guangzhou Fellowship. John spoke Mandarin and Cantonese fluently. He knew the Bible well. He had church planting experiences in HK, Taiwan, and the PRC. Between the main meeting and four sister meetings in Guangzhou, there were over 100 disciples to care for.

Lily and Yan Chi, whom we supported for two years, were financially stable. Lily bore good fruit for Jesus. God was gracious to her and to Yan Chi.

RCC adopted the Fanling Children's Meeting as a part of their Preacher's Department. Most of the children memorized Psalm 23. Five children memorized badge one which includes: John 3:16, John 1:12, John 14:6, Psalm 119:11 and Psalm 23. Some of the teenagers from RCC's youth group helped with this ministry. Others who helped us this month included: Jude O'Leary from Australia, Rheba Carter from the US, Luther and Helen from HK, Wai Na from HK, and Mary from South Korea. She hosted the meeting.

On November 25, a teenage boy believed in Jesus during a Fan Ling Wai children's meeting. After that, another child believed in Jesus as well. Our family was still involved.

The orphanage closed again to foreigners on November 27. The director said that this ban would last until the end of February 1996. At that time, we could reapply for entry. I returned unused funds to the donors. I did not ask for money for the orphans, but money was given.

Doors were shutting for me in Guangzhou. On the evening of December 6, after singing hymns with my family, the Lord put this prayer in my mouth, "Lord, You are the wise Master Builder. Please show us Your plan. What is Your blueprint? I know that a foreman plans a day's work before the workers arrive on site. Please give us Your instructions."

The Lord said of Abraham, "For I have known him, in order that he may command his children and his household after him, that they keep the way of the Lord, to do righteousness and justice, that the Lord may bring to Abraham what He has spoken to him." In Genesis 19, God judged the Sodomites with fire and brimstone. The parents of Sodom neglected to teach their children the ways of the Lord. They were too preoccupied with pleasing their flesh. They perished. The Lord called us to keep our own children's Christian upbringing a high priority.

The orphanage ministry was at its end. Lily and her baby were on their own. Lemuel took care of the Guangzhou ministry. We decided to purchase airline tickets for a furlough in the US.

On Christmas Eve, Grace, Glory and Andrew, along with their classmates sang at four events in HK. Two performances at a shopping mall in Sheung Shui! Another in an open space at a large housing estate! Two famous Christian celebrities performed with them at a mall, as did Christians from YFC. Over 50 unbelievers professed faith in Jesus that day. Glory to God!

On Christmas Day, my family, 15 students from RCC's student fellowship and six others joined Lemuel and me to serve at a wedding ceremony in Guangzhou. Lemuel officiated. I gave the message. Grace, Glory and Andrew sang at the banquet afterwards. About 70 people attended the evening service.

On December 26, Glory and Andrew sang with student fellowship members at the Yau Ling Kindergarten. 200 children attended this event. Praise the Lord!

~ Chapter 13 ~
Called by the Gospel (1996)

The Lord blessed us with money to return to the US. Two
Christians offered us use of their vans. Two Christians offered us
places to stay in their home. On January 10, we arrived in St.
Louis, where we were greeted by Sherry's parents, her siblings,
and by my brother. We stayed with Sherry's sister Sara.

Before we left HK, we gave the lease of our apartment to
another ministry. We distributed most of our belongings to the
missionary community, closed our mailbox, paid our bills, and
finalized our ministry responsibilities with RCC. We thanked the
Lord for YFC and RCC.

We must preach the Gospel and make disciples. This goal
was clear to us. We prayed that our children would love God and
His Word. We continued to teach Grace, Glory and Andrew their
daily ACE homeschool lessons.

Sherry often prayed, "Lord, let us bear a hundredfold fruit
for Your Name's sake." When we return to the PRC, we hope it
will be to work with an ACE school that has been established in
Guangzhou. In ACE home-schools, the Bible is taught throughout
the curriculum. We hoped to teach our children God's Word
while spreading His Word to others. We hoped to be close to the
Guangzhou orphanage.

Between February 16 – 20, we visited with Sherry's sister
and brother-in-law, Captains Jerry, and Louise Rowland. They

took us with them on their Sunday school pickup route. They did the route on Saturday to remind the children to come on Sunday and then, did the route again on Sunday. They invited us to share during their meetings at The Salvation Army of Marion, Indiana.

The Lord answered our prayers for a car. We purchased a 1990 Crown Victoria station wagon with low mileage and with seating capacity for eight people. It had a cargo carrier on top. This became useful for when we moved to our new home.

We shared with a small group of Life Christian Center Christians led by John and Jan Turnure. This couple was prepared to do mission work in Vietnam. We enjoyed the fellowship.

Pastor Paul Russell of Abundant Life Church offered his church as a location for us to start a work among Chinese people in St. Louis. St. Louis had over 35,000 Chinese people. It was a great offer, but I believed that we would return to the PRC.

Stephen Star offered me the position of Assistant Director of the Hide the Word in Your Heart Club. I thanked him but told him that I believed we would return to the PRC within a year. He responded by giving me the name of Grace Chapel in Houston, Texas. Grace Chapel was a congregation of Chinese Christians that was looking for an assistant pastor.

I did contact Grace Chapel about the position. Perhaps, the Lord did want us to work among the Chinese in the US. Senior Pastor Hong Sit invited me to preach, and afterwards, he and the leaders extended a call to me to pastor their English-speaking members. Sherry and I prayed for five days about the call, and then, confirmed a yes to Grace Chapel on March 28.

We moved to Katy, a suburb of Houston. The Star Family lived 15-minutes from us. We arrived on April 5. We enjoyed a Resurrection Day welcome at Grace Chapel on April 7.

Before settling in Houston, the Lord blessed us with four ministry opportunities. Sunday morning ministry at Living Faith Center, Ashland, Missouri! Weekday ministry among 300 hundred elementary and high school students at Christian Fellowship, Columbia, Missouri! Sunday morning ministry at Faith Family Chapel, Fayette, Missouri! Sunday morning ministry to over 40 Sunday school students at St. John's Evangelical Lutheran Church in LaPorte, Indiana! We praised Jesus for the privilege to be His witnesses.

The Lord answered Sherry's prayer for our children. She prayed especially for Andrew to have a backyard with a fence around it so that he could do his investigating without having to be watched every minute. In HK we had no backyard. While in Katy, Texas, we rented a brick house from elder Larry Leung of Grace Chapel. It had a tree in the front yard that the children enjoyed climbing and then, hanging out up there, plus a fenced in backyard.

During July 1995, Gary Ingram prophesied over me that I would pastor a Chinese church in the US within 18 months. As he spoke, I felt the presence of the Lord come over me like electricity. Here I was pastoring a Chinese church in the US.

Sherry taught junior-high-aged children their Sunday school lessons. I taught college-aged and new-career-aged adults their Sunday school lessons. On Friday evenings, I shepherded a youth group that ranged from 8 – 30 years-old. I preached to the English-speaking congregation on Sunday morning. During the week, I did outreaches to Chinatown and visited with people of the congregation. Sherry and I did VBS from June 3 – 7.

Pastor Larry and Mimi Leung pastored the Cantonese congregation at Grace Chapel. Pastor Luke and Esther Liang pastored the Mandarin congregation. I pastored the English-speaking Chinese. The founding and senior Pastor Hong Sit, and his wife Amy advised and prayed for us.

Amy Sit produced a CD of Scripture set to opera music. She invested $40,000 in this project. Channel 2 News in Houston did an interview with her about her CD. The arias are by such composers as Mozart, Dvorak, Verdi, and Puccini. The CD was done with the help of a symphony orchestra and a professional male tenor and female soprano. Amy raised $2,600 for Bibles for China through sales of this CD. She also produced a cassette tape with Scriptures set to well-known children's songs.

Grace, Glory and Andrew studied their ACE home-school curriculum under the supervision of Brother Rick Pinckney three days per week, and two days per week under our supervision. Brother Rick was better known as Happy Clown on the Hide the Word in Your Heart Club TV program. Evie Dawn, Mary Ruth, and Amy Grace of the Star Family were in Grace, Glory and

Andrew's class. They enjoyed eating the dewberries that grew there. Sherry and Mercy joined me at Grace Chapel while the older children were at school. Mercy played in the nursery and on the playground while Sherry maintained a protective eye on her.

While witnessing on April 19, our family met a Cantonese speaking Vietnamese woman (Ah Lan) in Chinatown. She received our Gospel tract and expressed interest to know more about Jesus. She told us that she never understood why Jesus was God and yet He died on the cross. She gave us her phone number. Later, she joined the fellowship meeting with Pastor Luke Liang.

On April 26, Grace, Glory, Andrew, and Amy Grace led a children's meeting in our front yard. They came up with the songs, Bible stories, testimonies, and special music. Grace did the altar call and two girls ages seven (Venessa) and nine (Amber) prayed to Jesus and professed faith in Christ. Grace exhorted them to ask God to forgive their sins at the end of each day. She said, "The Bible says that there is none righteous no not one. We all sin every day. So, we need to ask God to forgive us each night before we go to sleep." We were blessed to hear the Lord speak through her. Venessa, and her two friends, Andrew, and Cody, attended church with us yesterday. A third boy, Duane, woke up at four in the morning on Sunday in anticipation of joining us, but after he got in our car, he began to vomit. He had the flu. His Sunday clothes were a mess and he had to return home. He was so disappointed. Duane, Andrew, and Cody were brothers. Their parents worked. These boys spent a lot of time outside on their own. They were difficult to control but we included them.

Venessa practiced with Grace and Glory to sing for the Mother's Day service at Grace Chapel. Venessa progressed in her walk with Jesus. Amber, on the other hand, did not come back since the day she believed. She lived faraway.

On May 4, I went to a student barber school to get a haircut. I met a large group of Vietnamese and two Chinese people there. One Chinese lady was from Shanghai and the other from Guangzhou. As I shared about Jesus with Wanda (from Guangzhou), many Vietnamese students gathered around, so I interpreted for them what I was sharing with Wanda. Both ladies were interested to join the mid-week service at Grace Chapel.

Duane, Andrew, and Cody attended church with us. Duane and Venessa sang in church with Grace, Glory and Andrew on Mother's Day. Their parents appreciated our effort. On May 25, their father gave us free tickets to a game between the Astros and Cubs in the Astrodome.

Sherry reached out to a neighborhood lady named Linda. Linda used to be active in her church. Linda did not join Grace Chapel, but she did start attending her former church again. Linda gave us some kitchen items, a small pool for our children and a cassette tape of her singing. Sherry urged Linda to bring her son up in the ways of the Lord.

On May 26, the Lord gave me the precious opportunity to share the Gospel with an elderly lady from Guangzhou. She was diagnosed with stage-four cancer, with a tumor on her brain. I shared the Gospel with her in Cantonese. She repented of her sin and professed faith in Christ as her Lord and Savior.

I loaned Mrs. Tam a set of videos from Charles and Francis Hunter in Cantonese on divine healing. The tapes were interpreted by Pastor Sit and his wife Amy. We also tried to lead Mrs. Tam's son-in-law to Christ.

On June 3, we started free English classes. The classes were held in Chinatown at the Houston Community Police Station at 9146 Belliare Road. The police let me use a classroom with a seating capacity of 70 free-of-charge.

After I preached a message entitled, "Desperate for God's Kingdom," Ballwin Chin told me that God called him into ministry. He felt inadequate. Ballwin was an excellent Bible teacher. I placed my hand on his shoulder and prayed for him.

Grace Chapel was founded in 1956. The congregation's goal was to train and send American-born Chinese people to the PRC to preach the Gospel. They suffered major setbacks over the years but continued to press on with their mission.

Mercy Joy celebrated her fourth birthday this month. Mrs. Kimbro Dott provided a large Sara Lee Birthday cake for her party. Mercy received a baby doll and stroller for her birthday. She was a good mother to that baby doll.

On June 23, our son Andrew, his friends Dewayne and Venessa were baptized. Two Chinese believers, Ruth, and Sarah were also baptized. Praise the Lord!

The English class at the Chinatown Police Station grew from 2 – 20 students. Ballwin Chin, Johnson Fan, Pastors Larry, and Mimi Leung and Yohanna Tirayoh assisted with tutoring the students. I worked with Cantonese, Mandarin and Vietnamese speaking students. We taught them to sing Christian songs. Most of these students came to church services.

Sherry, the children, and I enjoyed weekly meetings in Chinatown with several new Vietnamese believers from the Monday evening English class. The meetings started at 4 pm. We also led meetings for Caucasians on Tuesdays at 10 am. This latter meeting was a fruit of the VBS ministry.

We shared with the Grace Chapel worship team Scripture songs that we learned at RCC. One song entitled, "Lord, I belong to You" was composed by Gary Shaw, one of our fellow missionaries. We wanted God's praise to be glorious.

Mrs. Tam went to be with Jesus 11 days after we shared the Gospel with her. Her daughter asked me to do the funeral service for her mother. The funeral took place on June 26. I sang, gave two messages in Cantonese (one during the funeral service and the other during the internment). A Baptist couple said it was the best funeral message that they had ever heard. They made a large donation to Grace Chapel. Glory to God!

Amy Sit taught Grace and Glory piano lessons. They let us use a synthesizer and overhead projector at home for rehearsals. Grace and Glory did short skits to help me illustrate my sermons.

The Celebrant Singers did a concert at Grace Chapel on August 7. The Singers were 26 Spirit-filled young people from Visalia, California. I worked with them before in HK and in the PRC. They also did a concert for orphans in Houston.

5 – 6 children rode with us on Sundays to Grace Chapel. Dwayne Stamp's brother, Andrew, believed in Jesus on August 25. Praise the Lord! Michael Trahan, Cody Walker and Jill Shehan started attending services with us. Michael's mother is Jewish. Cody loved to attend church. Venessa invited her mother and boyfriend to attend Grace Chapel.

I ministered to 35 – 40 people per week. The Elders and Deacons pressured me to increase attendance and financial offerings. I wondered why, because of the four pastors connected to Grace Chapel, the Lord was using me to lead people to faith, baptize them and add them to the Church.

Baldwin Chin took over the lead of the Young Adults Fellowship on Friday evenings. He led the young adults to study Romans. Baldwin was a prosecuting attorney. He knew how to ask questions that made people think. Baldwin's brother, Edwin, was a dentist. He was my prayer partner and advisor. He helped me with the mission program, the education department, the worship services, and discipleship among the men in the church.

Pastor Sit and Amy coached me on my sermon delivery. They asked me to memorize my message including all Bible verses so that I would focus on the people as I preach. Last week, as I memorized Scripture verses for my sermon, I found more meaning in them than before. I was more able to focus on eye-to-eye contact and gestures. Praise the Lord!

Grace, Glory and Andrew were happy at West Little York Church of God Accelerated Christian Education Academy. Their teachers included Judy Thompson and Rick Pinckney. Evie, Mary, Amy, and Melody Star attended this school. Our children were happy to have friends they knew at this school.

Sherry taught Sunday school classes for young teenagers. She learned how to word process on a computer so she could help me in the church office. She mowed the church lawn with the riding mower. She also helped me to clean the church. We started each day with prayer and worship in the church sanctuary.

I read a children's edition of the book, "The Hiding Place" to our children. The book was a good reminder about our need to forgive those who sin against us. Corrie was mistreated numerous times while imprisoned in a Nazi concentration camp. Despite the unpleasant circumstances, she kept giving and sacrificing for others rather than to turn inward and bitter. When she sacrificed, she experienced joy, revelation from God's Word and she could pray prayers of faith. When she became inward and selfish, her joy dried up. We read the stories of Evangelist Billy Sunday, Ida Scudder missionary to India and Jonathan Goforth missionary to China. God built a fire in us for His work through these books.

One night while considering the needs of the Guangzhou orphans, I received a fax from New Zealanders Ralph and Judy Duley. Their fax stated that there was a New Zealander named

Sandra King with an apartment 10-minutes from the orphanage. The orphanage authorities allowed her to minister to the orphans. This news was like a rainbow after a devastating storm. The next day, I composed orphanage ministry goals. One goal was to obtain the address of Sandra King. At that moment, the telephone rang. It was a missionary named Chris. He called to tell me that Lily's and his August 23 wedding went well. He proceeded to tell me that Lily was helping a lady named Sandra King with Guangzhou orphan ministry. He told me that he did not have Sandra's Guangzhou address on him but would send it to me. Wow! Praise God! Then, the next day, Sandra King's address was in our mailbox. Ralph and Judy Duley sent it to me.

Isaiah 58:6-9 came to mind, "Is this not the fast that I have chosen: to loosen the bonds of wickedness, to undo the heavy burdens, to let the oppressed go free, and that you break every yoke? Is it not to share your bread with the hungry, and that you bring to your house the poor who are cast out; when you see the naked, that you cover him, and not hide yourself from your own flesh? Then your light shall break forth like the morning, your healing shall spring forth speedily, and your righteousness shall go before you; the glory of the Lord shall be your rear guard. Then you shall call, and the Lord will answer; you shall cry, and He will say, 'Here I am.'"

On October 28, KLTJ TV in Houston asked me to share about the orphans in Guangzhou. I shared 20 slides. The first group of slides were pictures of orphans that we knew by name.

242

The second group of slides focused on volunteer services that our family and contacts did for the children. Two former missionaries to the PRC contacted me after they saw this telecast. One of them came to Grace Chapel on November 3.

It became clear to me that the Lord was calling me back to Guangzhou. Lydia in Guangzhou called to inform me of a teaching position that was open where her grandson attended school. The school was ready to hire me. By faith, I told the leaders at Grace Chapel that we were returning to the PRC. Thankfully, because of their hearts for the Lord and for the people of China, they were supportive.

By God's grace, we departed from Houston on December 9 and arrived in Guangzhou on December 10. I began to teach at a Chinese pre-school named Nations International School. The pay was $245 per month, plus accommodations, utilities and three meals per days except on weekends. I taught four hours per day. I prepared my lessons and taught our children during the remainder of the day. We lived 30-minutes from the Guangzhou orphanage.

David Chu and his wife Louise agreed to help Grace Chapel with the preaching ministry that I left behind. David was still the director of Youth for Christ, but he needed to physically reside in the US to complete his naturalization process for citizenship. The members of Grace Chapel were happy.

The pastoral staff and members of Grace Chapel sent us to China with their blessing. They were good to us. They paid us our full salary for December even though we left on December 9th.

The Lord miraculously provided for our needs. We needed $4,400 for our airline tickets. We received the needed funds just three days before the purchase date deadline. I was happy. Then, Sherry reminded me to tithe on the income. So, I took $440 tithe to Grace Chapel on a Wednesday. I took the tithe to the church office on Wednesday because I needed the Lord's return on the tithe that same day. When I gave the church secretary the $440, she told me that there was an envelope for me. When I opened it, there was $1,000 in the envelope. We now, had enough for the airline tickets and traveling money as well. Another blessing was that we sold most of our possessions during a yard sale.

The Lord prepared us through His Word for this transition. As I prepared a Sunday message, the Lord made it clear to me that the Kingdom of God and the kingdom of man flow in opposite directions. The kingdom of man flows toward self, whereas the kingdom of God flows towards God and others. There is no difference between a "Christian" and a "sinner" when their motives are both for self. Even a pastor or a Christian can covet spiritual things for his own sake, and not for the glory of God. The kingdom of man finds security in its possessions, power, and reputation, whereas Jesus became a servant of no reputation and placed obedience above His own life's value.

Jesus taught, "It is easier for a camel to go through the eye of a needle than for a rich man to enter the kingdom of God." [28]

---

[28] Mark 10:25

The eye of the needle is that short doorway in the city wall where a man must unload his camel's burdens before he can get his camel through that short entrance way. A rich man wants to hold onto his possessions and therefore is unable to follow Jesus in all the places Jesus goes.

Before we departed for Guangzhou, our family was blessed to take people with us to live performances of the play entitled, "Heaven's Gate. Hell's Flame." The script, the costumes, the scenery, and acting were excellent. Both nights, at least one third of the audience went forward to pray to Christ. Evangelist Bruce Thum and his daughter had done this play for many years. What a privilege it was to have a Cherokee Indian like him to share the Gospel with us. Jill and Brandon Shehan repented of their sins and believed in Jesus. Brandon did not attend the play, but his sister Jill felt compelled to bring him to Sherry. She told Sherry, "He wants his name to be written in the "Land's book of life." Sherry told Jill, "You mean the Lamb's Book of Life." Sherry, then, led Brandon through the sinner's prayer. Sherry also witnessed to another neighbor, asking him, "Is your name in the Lamb's Book of Life?"

Ray took us to the airport after he picked up Mary, Amy, and Melody Star along the way. They helped us carry our eight suitcases and eight carry-on bags to the airport. We appreciated their help. When we arrived at Kai Tak Airport in HK, our friend Annie Yun was waiting for us. She helped us to push our luggage carts to the airport bus stop.

We boarded the bus for the Kowloon Station. When we got off the bus, Tony Kanagbo helped me carry our luggage up the equivalent of four flights of stairs. This was a considerable blessing. Four of our suitcases weighed 70 pounds each. We transported a year's worth of ACE curriculum for our children, plus many books for teaching ABC's in the Guangzhou pre-school. Annie bought chicken legs with thighs, as well as drinks for the children. I purchased train tickets from HK to Guangzhou. We missed the last through-train to Guangzhou, so we ended up taking a through-bus to Guangzhou. The downside of taking the bus was that we had to unload and reload our luggage at the PRC border. The Lord graciously provided two men from the China Travel Service to help me unload and reload our luggage at the border. It was 7:30 pm local time when we met Lydia, her son-in-law, daughter, and grandson at the bus station. They brought a van large enough to move us and our luggage. After they fed us, they brought us to our new home. 39 hours after we left Houston, we reached our new home in Guangzhou at about 10 pm local time.

The Nations International School provided us a furnished apartment with four single beds, a queen-sized bed, a refrigerator, water heater, water boiler for drinking water, nice sofa, table, and chairs, two desks with chairs, a rice cooker, electric frying pan and three self-standing wardrobe cabinets. We lived on the fifth floor. The school had a high concrete wall around it which was painted with Disney characters (Lion King). There was a playground in the courtyard with four slides, two swing sets, a merry-go-around, monkey bars, large sand box, an unusable swimming pool and some Lil' Tikes houses.

I taught the pre-school children from 9:00-10:30 each morning and again from 6:00-6:30 in the evening. I taught four classes per day Monday – Thursday, and three classes on Fridays. Each lesson was 30-minutes in length. My preparation time was lengthy because I looked up as many as 30 words in a Mandarin dictionary per lesson. I wrote these words on flash cards, so I could practice saying them before each class. Most of my teaching was done in Mandarin because it was the official language of the PRC. Some students did not understand Cantonese. Sherry and the children helped me to teach the children. I used various methods to teach the children English including singing, picture story cards and activities.

Our challenges included a washing machine that needed repaired and a hot water heater that was unfaithful to heat. It was cold in our apartment. There was no internet available. We had no address in English to give our family and friends in the US, so, we enclosed address labels in Chinese with our outgoing letters for the recipients to attach to their envelopes when they wrote us back. I was concerned at first about the dependability of the PRC mail system, but soon after we sent out our first batch of letters, a steady stream of letters started flowing back to us.

Sherry wrote to her parents: "We purchased a space heater and hair dryer. We purchased long underwear for the children to use as pajamas. We purchased a wool-lined denim jacket for me. The jacket lining and hood are removable. It is a nice-looking jacket for only $27."

The principal's name was Mrs. Jia Shu Yue. She was from Beijing. She taught children for 37 years. She cooked eggs and sausage for us one morning. She bought us dishes. She started attending church services with Lydia and us.

Lydia and her son-in-law, Mr. Wu, obtained for us multi-entry visas so we could come and go from HK as needed. They were very good to us. We appreciated them very much.

There was an ACE school within walking distance from us. The leaders came to visit us. They told us that they would order new PACE workbooks for our children as needed.

~ Chapter 14 ~
Called by the Gospel (1997)

Sherry wrote to her parents, "We were tested and if it had not been for the Lord's tender mercies (His compassions never failing), we would have been utterly consumed. But glory to God, the devil lost again. The battle got so fierce at times that God was the only one who could fight, and He did so even while carrying us. The battle was the Lord's and now, the victory is ours. Praise the Lord! Great is His faithfulness!"

"All was going well and comfortable, then, on January 1, a day off, we visited a petting zoo. As we fed the donkeys, I felt an allergy attack coming on. That night, I came down with a severe earache. The next few days, I had a very painful sore throat. At 2 am on January 5, I was startled by flashing lights and when I opened my eyes, I had only tunnel vision. While the flashing lights took place, all I could see in my mind was the word, "Retreat!" I was not sure if this was from the Lord or the devil. I felt under fire. The following days, three expressions came to me: "A bruise reed shall He not break; a smoking flax shall He not quench, till He sends forth judgment unto victory... sometimes I felt like a candle that had already been blown out; and I also thought of a bird who had lost its song because of fear. I wanted my song back."

"On January 6, my glands all over my body began to ache. I felt extremely weak. For two weeks, I experienced a low-grade fever. I received a potent antibiotic for seven days intravenously at a nearby hospital as an outpatient [Sherry sat at a school desk in a large cold room with other patients. A needle was inserted into her arm each day and the very cold liquid was fed directly into her vein. It was very painful for her. She had to return daily for a week for this treatment.] Being so weak for so long, sudden fear and panic began to get the best of me. The Bible was my comfort. The Lord healed me on January 18. He strengthened my will to remain in the PRC for the sake of the Chinese people who need Him so badly. We are just going forward one day at a time."

"Grace is very helpful with Mercy. She sweeps and mops the floor without being asked. Much dust accumulates daily. Since, we've been here, she said, "I am learning to sacrifice, be patient and pray. I was happy when I saw my friend Anna."

"Glory said, 'I learned that the children at this school are sweet. They give a lot of kisses and need a lot of love. I am very happy to love them. The most fun I had was when we went to HK and stayed at our friend, Anna Grave's, home. We built forts.'"

"Andrew could not think of anything to say. On December 31 evening, while playing in the sand, a child threw so much sand in his eyes that he could not even shut his eyes. He could see nothing. We rinsed his eyes immediately, but to no avail. Mark, Yu Zhang, and the school cook took turns carrying Andrew and thus, rushed him to a nearby hospital on foot. A doctor there used sixteen long-stemmed Q-tips to carefully absorb the sand out from under his eyelids. Then, the doctor flushed Andrew's eyes with a special solution. It was painful, but Andrew was happy to see again. Jesus was merciful to him. He has had no problems with his eyes since that day. Praise God! Andrew is usually thoughtful, loving, and helpful. We thank the Lord for him."

"Mark has been remarkable! A true best friend! He is a very gentle teacher with the school children and yet, our children do not doubt that they have first place in his heart."

After Sherry told me that the Lord impressed on her to remain committed to the ministry in Guangzhou, we visited Lydia, and told her about it. She was happy. I told her that the reason I had thought to take Sherry back to the US was that she was my best friend, and leaving China was the way I could lay down my life for her. Jesus said, "Greater love has no man than this, that a man lay down his life for his friend." Then, Lydia replied with a kind smile, "Sherry is the one who laid down her life for her friend. She has followed you here for 10 years, raised your four children and suffered many times so you could preach the Gospel to the Chinese." I nodded my head in agreement and endeavored to show more respect to Sherry.

On January 24, Sherry, the children, and I had a part in a parents' and children's meeting at the pre-school. They did choreography to a song entitled, "Lord, I Lift Your Name on High" using a soundtrack with the words in Cantonese. They did another song entitled, "It's a Miracle!" This is a song they learned from the Star Family. We sang a song entitled, "Mercy." Amy Sit wrote this song for our daughter Mercy. Some of the lyrics are,

"God is good! God is kind! God delights in mercy, Oh, satisfy me, with Thy mercy, oh Lord." The song was sung to the melody of Brahms's lullaby. There were two police officers in attendance because their children attended this school. The Lord led us to be bold and not silent. Jesus may return soon.

On January 29, the temperature dipped down to 48 degrees. The air was damp, so it felt colder than 48. Also, we had nowhere to retreat from the cold. We had a small space heater, but usually only turned it on at night or during baths and showers. Our apartment was not heated. Sherry and the children had to wear several layers of clothes to stay warm. Sherry wore two to three layers of thermals and slacks.

On February 16, a new hope dawned. After two miserably cold and rainy weeks, we received a call from Sandra King. A Chinese mother wanted to give a baby to her. Sandra needed me to interpret. The adoption had to be done in a simple but legal fashion. On February 17, I helped with this process. The mother was too poor to raise the child but wanted her baby to receive good care. Sandra asked me to carry the baby. When we reached Sandra's home, I handed the baby over to Sherry. Her heart was captivated by this little one. Her name was Dawn. Her estimated date of birth was February 8, 1997. Sherry's birthday is February 8. Wow! Sandra reported the abandoned child to the appropriate authorities. They consented to Sandra's care of baby Dawn.

From February 23 – 28, Sandra asked us to care for Dawn while she was on a business trip. We enjoyed living in her village.

252

The Christians invited us to attend their church. At their church, they had a leader who helped illiterate members to memorize the lyrics of hymns before the worship began. This was so they could sing with the congregation.

The mountains that surrounded the village reminded us of Jerusalem. Grace said, "Every time I look at them, I remember the Scripture, 'I will lift-up mine eyes to the mountains from where does my help come from? My help comes from the Lord most high who made heaven and earth.'" Andrew liked it because he caught five iguanas, and a neighbor gave him a snapping turtle and a dragon lizard. Andrew also liked to fish in the lake.

We were granted permission to visit the government-run orphanage again. Praise the Lord! This news came to us unexpectedly. We asked the Lord to lead us in this regard.

The Guangzhou Grace Academy offered our children 50% off tuition to enroll in their school. Normally, the tuition fee per child at this school was $10,000 per child. The leaders provided $15,000 from their scholarship fund for Grace, Glory and Andrew. They asked me to teach Physical Education for four hours per week to compensate for the rest of the fee.

International schools in the PRC charge this much because the cost of setting up and operating a high-standard school was extremely high. Grace prayed that she could attend this school. Lily had been praying for our children to get into this school. Thanks be to the Lord for His mercy! Sherry and I really liked the

ACE curriculum because it combined building Christ-like character along with a high-quality academic education.

On March 5, the China Daily published an article criticizing the US. The article was two pages long. Normally, page four of this publication was devoted to bashing the US. The Chinese leaders envisioned a new world order. These reports caused me concern because in June HK would revert to being property of the PRC. As I prayed about this, I envisioned a plant growing roots downward and growing a stem, branches, leaves, and blossoms upward. I took this vision to represent our need to keep rooting ourselves in Christ via Bible study, prayer, and obedience, and to impart to others the fruit of Christ in our lives. I also saw a cross. The journey towards the cross takes total faith. In the path of the cross, the Lord upholds, blesses, and makes us fruitful, even though it may seem that we are perishing.

By God's grace, I got to talk with Chan Ling, Yiht Wai, Hoi Syuhn, Bunbun and various other orphans in the Guangzhou orphanage. I did not get to see Ho Sui Kam or Taan Fa because their dorm was off limits. Bak Lam offered to take my greetings to them. The good news was that they had a new facility and their living conditions had improved.

Baby Dawn was well. Sandra was given a 14-month-old who had cerebral damage from birth, bronchitis, and an enlarged liver. She was also given a 10-year-old who had numerous epileptic seizures around the clock. Twice, Sherry stayed overnight to care for these children, so Sandra could rest.

I thanked the Lord for Dr. Young Yang because just before we left the US, he had a stopover in Houston, and at that time, he returned to me the ACE animal picture story cards and teaching manuals that I had given to him back in 1990. I never expected to receive these materials back, but this was the curriculum I used to teach the preschoolers. I used every bit of this curriculum. I translated over 1,000 English words from this material into Chinese characters. I only translated English words into Chinese that I could not recognize by sight. Having the children sing songs in English helped them to learn pronunciation. Louise, Sherry's sister, also gave us a cassette tape entitled, "First Sunday Singalong." From this tape, the children learned the Christian songs like, "The Wiseman Built His House." Sherry and the children did skits based on the parables of Jesus to teach the children English words. We also taught the children five Scripture songs with actions from Amy Sit's "Sing It" cassette tape. The song titles were, "Wisdom is the Principal Thing," "A Merry Heart, A Joyful Heart," "Even a Fool" (who keeps silent is counted wise), "Love not Sleep," and "He Brought Me to His Banqueting Table." We printed the words to these songs in large fonts on poster boards. I considered my efforts greatly rewarded when two of my students asked, "Is it true that Jesus died, rose from the dead and is coming again, and that He sees everything we are doing now?" A local television station felt my teaching methods were worth airtime. They videotaped me teaching the children English. Praise the Lord!

Lemuel faithfully ministered to the Guangzhou Christians on a weekly basis. We attended three meetings. We did not attend more often because Lemuel was shepherding the group. We were focused on our new ministry.

Principal Shu Ye and Lydia hoped we would never leave China. The PRC granted us resident visas to work and live for a year with multi-entry privileges mostly through their efforts. Wonderful! However, as we continued to teach Scripture songs and preach the Gospel to the children in this school, we knew that our privilege to remain in the PRC was at risk. The school was located between a military base, police station and a courthouse. The soldiers did outdoor workouts at 6:30 am and 6:30 pm daily.

Between April 1 – 11, letters sent to us from the US were returned to senders. This was because the school only paid for three-months of mail delivery service. They did not renew the service when it expired on March 31. The post office gave no prior notice. On April 12, the school renewed the mail delivery for us until the end of June. After that, we received letters again.

I shared a word of warning to those who wrote letters to us. Recently, a missionary was arrested when a postal worker saw that Bibles had been posted to him from outside of the PRC. The postal worker informed the police. I asked our contacts to use wisdom as to what they wrote within and without their envelopes. We made specials trip to HK to mail our newsletters to them.

The Nations International School offered me a 150% raise ($625 per month plus housing, utilities, and food). They offered to buy our return tickets from the US, if we came back after the summer break. The Fanling Christian Academy leadership offered us the whole school including an apartment if we took over that operation. We would also receive $2,000 per month pay. These were amazing offers. We prayed about these offers.

I taught two hours of Physical Education at the ACE school on Wednesday and Friday afternoons. Brian and Maria Hutt told us that next year there would be no free tuition for our children because there was no more money remaining in the scholarship fund. We thanked the Lord for the free months for which they did get to attend this school. We also thanked God that via Brian and Maria we learned of a worship service for foreigners in Guangzhou. We enjoyed attending that service. While there, we met Americans who were in the process of adopting children from the Guangzhou orphanage.

On May 1, Lydia's children took us to a private resort for wonderful Chinese cuisine and fishing. Andrew caught a lot of crabs. We swam in a public pool where there were water slides.

May 1 – 2, were public holidays in the PRC to honor the working class. We witnessed no public display of celebration. We did meet a taxi driver who told us that he was fined $5,000 for having a second child. His wife was forcibly sterilized. He told us that a friend of his was fined $10,000 for having a third child. A high official told us that he did not like the policy because his only child had a fatal disease and would eventually die.

On May 3, we learned that the Nation International School would be taken over by new owners. Major changes were underway. We had no idea that this would happen, but in my heart, I felt that June would be our last month.

The children enjoyed my classes. They gave me a hero's welcome when I entered the classrooms. Jesus was the real hero. A fellow missionary named Wendy took my teaching position.

During the last Guangzhou Christian Fellowship meeting that we attended, two sisters named Hau, and Huang testified of 98 salvations in a village where they preached. I gave them three briefcases of Bibles, Gospel tracts and hymnals. They were happy to receive them. Many Bible couriers had been arrested in recent days, so Bibles were hard to come by.

When the Chinese Christians prayed about our return to the US, they told us, "Do not say that you are going back to America, but the rather, you are being SENT to America. You are on a mission and God has a purpose for you to go there."

On June 8, I took part in baptizing four converts at a hotel. They were baptized in the hotel pool while other swimmers watched. I said the prayer of blessing. After that, we had a banquet and then, our weekly Christian meeting (at a different location). Grace. Glory and Andrew sang John 3:16 in Cantonese. I shared briefly about the importance of eternal values as opposed to temporary ones. Local believers gave us $1,000 in offerings during the last month, otherwise, we would have returned to the

US penniless. We committed our financial need to the Lord, and He provided. "Thank You Jesus!"

Grace, Glory and Andrew graduated from their courses at the Guangzhou Grace Academy on June 12. Grace did a ribbon choreography to the song, "Celebrate Jesus." Glory did two songs with the help of accompaniment soundtracks. One was a ballet-type duet with her good friend Aletha Hutt, and the other was a country and western Christian song. Glory lip synced the song, while other students stood behind her pretending to play musical instruments and did backup vocals. Andrew and the other students his age started the ceremony with a medley of worship songs to which they did choreography. We praised JESUS for a Christian ACE academy in the PRC.

There was a great need for Christian education in the PRC. The government banned religious education for children under the age of 18. I could share Biblical moral values but was not to mention the Name of Jesus. I had colorful Bible story books to give to my students but was forbidden to distribute them.

Sandra King took in four more abandoned children. These children had special needs. Sandra had locals serving as cook, administrator, and caregivers. Baby Dawn was healthy and happy.

We had several meetings with the new owners of the Nations International School. Wendy and Joseph Xu took over my position. They were fine Christians and friends of ours.

Our journey back to the US began at 4 am (3 am CST) on June 16, 1997. Lydia's family arranged transportation for us to the bus station. Two Chinese teachers, the principal, Lydia, Mercy, Yu Zhang, two grandsons, the school cook, and a van driver accompanied us to the station. Before we boarded the bus, we took photos. Good wishes, hugs, and handshakes were exchanged. After we boarded the bus, there was repeated hand waves. Tears were flowing! Finally, the bus took off for HK.

The journey to HK took almost four hours. At about 9:30 pm, we arrived at Lemuel's home where we stayed the night. We enjoyed fellowship with them until about 11 pm and then, went to sleep. The next morning at 6:30 am, I began to read my Bible and pray. By 8:30 am, missionaries Julian and Monica Hawkens came to see us. We enjoyed a time of fellowship with them. At 10 am, we began the journey to the airport.

At 12:15 pm, we boarded the Korean Airline 747-300B to begin our flight to America. We had stopovers in Seoul, Korea, Los Angeles, Dallas, Atlanta and finally, arrived in Tampa. After arriving in Dallas, we were welcomed by cousins of Sherry's mother, John, and Faye Kautt. Their son-in-law, Dennis also helped us with the luggage. Major Roy Rowland of The Salvation Army paid for our family's airline tickets from Dallas to Tampa. Otherwise, we would have ridden a Greyhound bus for nearly 30 hours rather than a short five-hour flight. May the Lord bless all these for what they have done. We went to Tampa because Sherry was battling middle ear infections in both ears as well as fever, dizziness, weakness, and achiness. The plan was for her to get some needed rest at her parents' home.

~ Chapter 15 ~
Called by the Gospel (Conclusion)

"The term Gospel comes from the Greek word that means 'good news.' In the Bible, the good news is what God has done for us in Jesus Christ. All His promises of grace, mercy, and eternal life are freely given to us through faith in Jesus." [29]

After we returned to the US in June of 1997, the Lord was faithful to open doors for me to share the love of Jesus with others. I served as an outreach coordinator with The Salvation Army of St. Petersburg, Florida. During that season, I did more than 200 visits with people in the neighborhood.

Later, between 2005 – 2020, we worked for The Salvation Army as officers. We did many charitable deeds for people in the communities where we lived. We inherited many wonderful Christian brothers and sisters as friends. Lost souls believed in Jesus at some locations, but far too few from my perspective.

One day, while living in the San Bruno, and working in the South Market District of San Francisco, California, I picked up a book entitled, "Called by the Gospel." It was a divine moment. Praise the Lord! That's it! I knew my soul was restless, but I could not put my finger on what was going on inside of me. Those four words reminded me that my original calling from the Lord was to focus on bringing the Gospel to lost souls.

---

[29] Middendorf, P. Michael and Schuler, Mark, Called by the Gospel, an Introduction to the New Testament, Wipf & Stock, 199 w. 8th Ave., Suite 3, Eugene, OR 97401

I like what the Lord did through Billy Graham. He turned non-church venues into venues to preach the Gospel to lost souls. For example, He preached the Gospel to lost souls at the Raymond James Stadium in Tampa Bay before the Buccaneers played their first football game in it. Thousands of souls streamed to their knees in repentance and professed faith in Christ during the days of that crusade. Praise the Lord!

The Lord says, "Those who are wise shall shine like the brightness of the firmament, and those who turn many to righteousness like the stars forever and ever." The true stars of this life turn people to righteousness. The primary objective that that the Lord Jesus has given to me as a servant of His Church is to seek and save the lost. This is my hope and prayer. More lost souls to hear the Gospel. More new professions of faith in Jesus Christ. Let us pray for revival!